NATIONAL AND FOREST PARKS

1. Puketi Forest
2. Waipoua Forest
3. Trounson Kauri Reserve
4. Coromandel Forest Park
5. Pirongia Forest Park
6. Pureora Forest Park
7. Te Urewera National Park
8. Egmont National Park
9. Whanganui National Park
10. Tongariro National Park
11. Abel Tasman National Park
12. Kahurangi National Park
13. Nelson Lakes National Park
14. Paparoa National Park
15. Arthur's Pass National Park
16. Westland/Tai Poutini National Park
17. Aoraki/Mt Cook National Park
18. Mt Aspiring National Park
19. Fiordland National Park
20. Catlins Forest Park
21. Rakiura National Park

CH00956558

Farewell Spit

Collingwood

TASMAN BAY

Heaphy Track

Motueka

Karamea

Nelson

Picton

Marlborough Sounds

Westport

Buller River

Reefton

Kaikoura Ranges

Punakaiki

Lewis Pass

Greymouth

Kaikoura

Hokitika

Arthur's Pass

TASMAN SEA

Okarito Lagoon

Torlesse-Craigieburn Drylands Park

Motunau Island

Franz Josef Glacier

SOUTHERN ALPS

Fox Glacier

Rakaia Gorge

CHRISTCHURCH

Aoraki/Mt Cook

Banks Peninsula

Jackson Bay

Haast

L. Pukaki

L. Takapo

Ashburton

Lake Ellesmere

Haast Pass

L. Ohau

Fairlie

Rangitata River

Mt Aspiring

L. Hawea

Twizel

Mackenzie Basin

Timaru

L. Wanaka

Omarama

PACIFIC OCEAN

Milford Sound

Wanaka

L. Wakatipu

Waitaki River

Queenstown

Cromwell

Oamaru

FIORDLAND

Alexandra

L. Te Anau

Te Anau

Clutha River

Otago Peninsula

L. Manapouri

Manapouri

DUNEDIN

Gore

Balclutha

Invercargill

Catlins

Codfish Island

FOVEAUX STRAIT

Curio Bay

Oban

N

Stewart Island

wild New Zealand

FROM THE ROAD

Otira Gorge, Arthur's Pass

wild New Zealand
FROM THE ROAD

written & photographed by
GORDON ELL

RANDOM HOUSE
NEW ZEALAND

Mt Ruapehu in eruption 1996

CONTENTS

The upper Waimakariri, Canterbury,
a braided riverbed.

THE ACCESSIBLE
WILDERNESS

Around a third of New Zealand's area is held in public reserves, a many-faceted wilderness that has increasingly been opened up to travellers in the past generation. While the wilderness of mountains, rivers, volcanoes, forests and coasts is still a physical challenge for most people, it is now possible to experience a good portion of it from the road.

The thrust of this account is to display the great variety of landscapes, the nature and wildlife that makes them special, and suggest ways to find and enjoy their wild places. The policy emphasis on developing short walks of an hour or two, springing from the roadside, has helped many more to enjoy the outdoors. Paths lead to features such as giant trees, waterfalls, lakes, and to seal and bird colonies. While the farther mountains remain a mystery, and only for the most adventurous, the 'front country' is somewhere people of all ages can experience wilderness.

The chance to see rare and endangered plants and birds are part of this record.

The traveller by road can plan a tour through different parts of the country, and find an introduction to its nature. Some journeys may be long and the traveller may prefer to camp (or find accommodation) before making wilderness forays. Others may enjoy taking walks into the parks as a break in a journey.

The Department of Conservation, which administers most of the wilderness, produces excellent pamphlets and local guides, available at local park headquarters. Much of it is also downloadable from www.doc.govt.nz.

Maps are more of a problem as in 2010 the national mapping service is changing the gridlines, and consequently their coordinates, to match the technology of GPS systems. The old maps are still useable but not for search and rescue. *The Penguin Atlas of New Zealand* provides road information with State Highway numbers in 1:250,000 scale but it is a large-format book. The 50,000 map series and park maps are often more useful for choosing minor roads off the beaten track.

The photographs and information in this book have been garnered over many years. Many of the journeys were originally taken on field trips, with colleagues from the Royal Forest and Bird Protection Society, and the various nature advisory committees I've been privileged to serve on.

During that time, the burgeoning travel industry has brought 'civilisation' to most parts of the country. Places which once required a day's tramp, or hitching a ride

with the local boatman or truck driver, can now be explored from the road by a range of sophisticated tourist services.

While the fascination of discovering remote places and nature for oneself has been compromised by passing years, the increased opportunities to access our wild places from the road continues to delight.

These journeys begin at major travel nodes in the North Island (Auckland) and Marlborough. It introduces loop journeys around Northland, the Bay of Plenty, the central North Island, and travelling south down either side of the island. In the South Island it heads inland to Nelson, or down the east coast to Canterbury and Otago, as far as Stewart Island and back up the West Coast. Drive either way, take a trip to your preferred region, or make up a figure of eight exploration.

▲ *ABOVE: Introduced weeds and wildflowers are a feature of New Zealand's roadsides. Plantings of Russell lupins are common in the dun landscapes of the South Island high country.*

For the benefit of those unfamiliar with New Zealand's origins 80 million years ago, as a splinter off the ancient continent of Gondwana, the chapter 'New Zealand's Wild Heritage' looks at the evolution of its strange natural history. New Zealand's isolation before the evolution of mammals is just one aspect of this account of the last place on earth (barring the Antarctic) to be occupied by people. It is such factors, including the first human settlement as recently as 800–1000 years ago, that shape the wilderness and nature we have today.

Go, explore, discover and enjoy.

NEW ZEALAND'S WILD HERITAGE

The peculiar natural history of New Zealand is the product of its isolation from the rest of the world. Its unusual birds, its ancient trees and plants, the primitive life forms all evolved far from other lands, and without the interference of humans, or any of the four-legged predators.

Apart from some small bats, there were no land mammals in ancient New Zealand, hence its popular description as a 'land of birds'. Many bird species evolved to occupy niches inhabited in other countries by four-legged animals. Giant and flightless moa took the place of grazing animals; kokako wattlebirds swooped from treetop to treetop, feeding along the branches much like squirrels do elsewhere; the ground-dwelling kiwi and weka probed for their food like badgers and pigs; tiny wrens and robins occupied the niches inhabited elsewhere by small animals such as mice and voles.

The impact of the first humans, who arrived less than a thousand years ago, was catastrophic on this land and its nature. Maori burnt much of the forest cover, creating open land for hunting and for grubbing fern root. Their dogs chased the birds; rats ate them. So did Maori. Within a century or two, many gargantuan and flightless birds, such as moa, became extinct. Some 32 bird species disappeared in Maori times.

The arrival of European settlers barely 200 years ago and their introduction of European mammals further disrupted this delicate balance. In European times a further 11 bird species were lost and populations of the survivors plunged, sometimes critically. In European times another 40 percent of the forest gave way to farms and towns. The very nature of the country changed; many habitats simply vanished. Ninety percent of the wetlands were lost as farmers cleared the forest and swamps from the rich riverflats.

The process continues today with the intensification of agriculture, particularly dairying with its stupendous demands for water and its frequent pollution of waterways. At the same time, burgeoning housing developments threaten sensitive coastal environments.

Fortunately, New Zealand has a magnificent heritage of parks and reserves, covering more than a third of the country. This is the wild New Zealand celebrated in this book.

These wild places are not like the original forests and waterways. The introduction of various exotic animals, for sport or speculation, has created a new dynamic even in the protected forests. The brush-tailed possum, introduced from Australia in the 1880s as a possible source of commercial furs, has proven a major threat to forests, successively killing out several kinds of forest trees, their 'ice cream plants'. Gaunt skeletons of the red-flowering rata and pohutukawa are among the victims. To the vegetation-browsers, add different species of deer, chamois, thar and goats which have severely damaged many forests and high-country environments.

Feral cats, dogs and rats take their toll of birds and their nests. Hedgehogs eat the eggs of ground-nesting birds. Rabbits have historically devastated vast areas of dry grassland, to the extent that only introduced weeds will grow in places where the native grasses have been ravaged. Mustelids — ferrets/polecats, stoats and weasels — introduced to control the rabbits have moved further into the wild where they feed on birds. Even introduced insects have had a devastating effect in places: in summer the buzz of introduced wasps can be heard in the beech forests of the south as these insects in their millions take the honeydew produced on the tree trunks by scale insects, thus reducing the food available for native honey-eating birds.

None of this is obvious to the casual visitor to the forest but it is of major concern to the caretakers of our wilder-ness. It has been estimated that introduced pests (and invasive weeds) cost the New Zealand economy more than $840 million in 1999, or about one percent of the gross national product. Government and local authorities spend around $440 million each year in an attempt to keep pests and weeds in check.

Visitors from overseas sometimes comment on the local emphasis on 'killing' in the name of conservation. The justification for this approach is that our natural environment evolved without these pests, and its key elements cannot survive without some help. Wild New Zealand today is considerably modified from the world originally encountered by the first Polynesians. By any standard, however, what is left is a magnificent showcase of the primeval world.

Pest eradication on several offshore islands has recreated the pre-mammalian environment, enabling endangered birds to re-establish. Several species have been relocated or 'translocated' to spread and enhance populations. In other places the local removal of pests and weeds has allowed remnant populations to flourish.

While most of these special places are remote from the mainland, and closed to the general public, there are a few reserves specially maintained so the public can see rare birds living in the wild. These 'Open sanctuaries' and closely managed 'main-land islands' offer the best opportunities to see threatened, rare and endangered birds in more natural conditions.

The open sanctuary of Tiritiri Matangi Island near Auckland is the public showplace for this restoration. Accessible from the city by ferry, its wild popu-lations include saddleback, stitchbird, kiwi, notornis/takahe, parakeets, white-head, rifleman, brown teal and other rare or endangered native birds. Kapiti Island near Wellington is another accessible island sanctuary with similar birds, and

NEW ZEALAND'S 'DINOSAUR FORESTS'

Podocarps belong to the cone-bearing tree families which developed during the Age of Dinosaurs, 190–135 million years ago. New Zealand has several species of these ancient trees which are among the largest in the rainforest.

The campaigning British botanist Dr David Bellamy has described our lowland forests as 'dinosaur forests' because podocarps first evolved when those giant creatures roamed the earth.

New Zealand has 17 species of podocarps, mostly forest giants; these species include totara, rimu, kahikatea, pygmy pine, matai and miro. The kahikatea is the tallest, a podocarp which can reach 60 metres in height. New Zealand's smallest tree is also a podocarp; the pygmy pine usually grows to only 10–30 cm in height.

Many species are known in English as 'pines'. For example: rimu is also known as red pine; kahikatea as white pine; miro is brown pine, and matai black pine. Others are simply silver-yellow pine, yellow pine and bog pine.

The Latin word *Podocarpus* is a clue to this family of trees. The words mean fleshy-footed seed. All podocarps bear this kind of fruit — the tiny black seed is set on the end of a small, colourful berry which attracts birds to feed.

allows the survival of sensitive and vulnerable bird species on the mainland. The more accessible places include Trounson Kauri Park (Northland), Boundary Stream (inland Hawke's Bay), and St Arnaud (Nelson Lakes National Park).

Public restoration initiatives include the community-initiated Karori Wildlife Sanctuary, Zealandia, where a valley of 250 hectares is fenced off against pests and contains kiwi, only 10 minutes from Parliament Buildings in Wellington (page 164). Pukaha/Mt Bruce Wildlife Reserve in Wairarapa is run by a combination of the Department of Conservation and community volunteers (pages 120–121). Forest and Bird is restoring Bushy Park, inland from Whanganui (page 156). The local community has financed a pest-excluding fence around 3200 hectares of Maungatautari mountain in South Waikato in another community initiative.

The strange and ancient nature of New Zealand began to develop around 80 million years ago when these islands began their drift away from the shores of the great southern continent of Gondwana. These fragments detached from the Australian coast before the evolution of most mammals and flowering plants. Traces of the ancient life forms of those times can still be found in the nature of many New Zealand plants, and in primeval animals such as the tuatara, the native frogs, perhaps the geckos, and the weta.

Modern science has revealed how several continents were born of Gondwana: Australia, Africa, South America, Antarctica and the subcontinent of India have all drifted apart from the original Gondwana landmass. Their previous connection can be traced in their rocks,

particularly resident kaka bush-parrots. A range of other islands under restoration may be accessible from time to time: check with the Department of Conservation.

'Mainland islands' offer another opportunity to see endangered birds: these are discrete areas where intensive pest control

and in similar ancient plants that survive as fossils or related forests to this day. Relatives of our southern beech, for example, are found in eastern Australia, Tasmania and South America, and as fossils in Antarctica. These trees, like the native pines, date from the days of dinosaurs when plants reproduced from cones not flowers.

The kahikatea, once called the white pine, is probably the oldest with an evolutionary history estimated at 120 million years. Totara, rimu, kauri and celery pine are other ancient species. Among the

▲ *ABOVE LEFT, TOP AND BOTTOM: Podocarps (native pines) evolved before flowering plants. Their Latin/scientific name derives from their 'fleshy-footed seeds'.*

▲ *ABOVE RIGHT, TOP AND BOTTOM: Southern beech is an ancient forest-type predominant in the south and at higher altitudes. It reproduces by way of tiny cones not flowers.*

ancient ferns, the *Cyathea* tree ferns also date biologically from Gondwana days; but they are also found in South Africa, Australia and New Caledonia.

There is scientific argument that some

THE NORTHERN FORESTS

The warmer forests of northern New Zealand include a number of fine trees which don't grow naturally elsewhere. These include the coastal pohutukawa with its red blossoms at Christmas, the giant kauri, the celery pine or tanekaha, the leathery-leaved taraire, puriri, and a wealth of warmth-loving shrubs such as whau and puka. Mangroves, which are killed by frost, grow only in the north.

▲ *ABOVE: The tall-trunked mamaku or black tree fern is one of the ferns originating from the days of the dinosaurs. Its dark trunk is shaped with a diamond pattern. The national emblem, the ponga or silver fern, is also one of this ancient Cyathea family.*

of these plants and trees, ancient as their origins may be, found their way here after New Zealand became a separate land mass. Molecular biologists are presently working through the DNA of several species, including the southern beeches, to see if their ancestors really did drift here on the original New Zealand land mass, or whether they came later across the seas from distant neighbours. The evidence of fossil pollens shows continuity of some plants from Gondwanan times, but New Zealand's subsequent immersion in the ocean and its later uplifting has encouraged the alternative view — that the original species became re-established when the country assumed its present state.

In brief, the ancient subcontinent of Zealandia reached its present position about 60 million years ago, after a spell with a tropical climate. The land was largely immersed in the oceans, around 25 million years ago, becoming a scattered chain of islands. The emerging new land uplifted the submarine deposits so that sedimentary rocks form three-quarters of the present land mass. The emerging land was twisted and torn as a chain of high mountains rose along an alpine fault formed between eight and six million years ago. This fault, caused by the collision of two great earth plates (the Pacific and the Indo-Australian plates) is still shaping New Zealand.

The ice ages further carved the landscape, burying much of the country as far north as Tongariro. At the peak of the ice, some 20,000 years ago, seawater levels were much lower so the North and South islands were linked together with Stewart Island in one land mass. When the ice melted between 10,000 and 12,000 years ago, the sea rose up and drowned much of the lower coast, making islands and peninsulas of places like the Bay of Islands, the Hauraki Gulf and the Marlborough Sounds.

Throughout the ages, volcanoes also forged new landscapes as New Zealand rode the dynamic boundary between the vast Pacific Plate and the Indo-Australian Plate. Mountain building and vulcanism are dramatic processes still widely apparent in the landscape.

Whatever emerges from the scientific debates, one thing is already clear. New Zealand has been isolated geographically from the rest of the world for millions of years, and is indeed the last place in the world (barring Antarctica) to be settled by humans. That is what makes its wildlife and plants unique and a journey of discovery through it so fascinating.

The islands of New Zealand lie in the path of the Roaring Forties as they sweep unimpeded around the southern ocean. Not suprisingly it is a windy country,

The prevailing winds are westerly but with variations from the south and north generated as the anticyclones of the southern Pacific sweep by.

These winds also bear the rains — more than 8000 mm falls on Fiordland each year. As the prevailing winds climb the western slopes of the South Island, they drop their oceanic rain load, creating the wet environment of the West Coast rainforests. Then the winds spill over the peaks of the Southern Alps, descending as hot, drying air to create the dry high-country basins and sunburnt plains of the east. In contrast to Fiordland's rain, as little as 300 mm falls on Central Otago.

Similar west–east climate changes can be traced in the North Island where peak rainfall in the west varies from 1200–1800 mm and the east coast, protected by mountain ranges, is again drier.

The coastline is long and indented in many places. These small islands have as much coastline as the continental United States. Nowhere is far from the sea; the maximum distance is 110 kilometres.

At any time cold winds borne up from the Antarctic currents can bring wintry conditions, particularly to the South Island. Tropical storms and currents sweep down from the north, bringing subtropical conditions to favoured places. Thus New Zealand has three major climatic zones along its 1600 kilometres length. These help shape the nature of each region.

In the north, from about Auckland and the Bay of Plenty fringe, plants which are frost-tender, such as the mangrove, can grow. In the broad middle zone mixed rainforests flourish, as they do throughout New Zealand. In the south, there is a cooler region regularly affected by the subantarctic weather.

Altitude, too, plays a large part in the distribution of plants throughout these regions: the species which favour mountaintops in the north may grow nearer sea level in the south.

All this physical variation produces a rich range of habitats, from seashore to mountaintop, and from north to south.

The peculiar wildlife and nature of each of these regions are explored in this book.

AUCKLAND

AUCKLAND

Considering the country's largest city as a wild place may seem a little odd. The shape of the land, however, and its climate, create an environment where wilderness flourishes close to the city. Its great harbours, neighbouring mountains and forest remnants provide rich experiences for the visitor by car.

Auckland sprawls across a narrow isthmus, where the Pacific Ocean and the Tasman Sea almost meet, and where their tidal creeks deeply penetrate the land. The actual gap between the two seas (and tidal systems) is barely a kilometre near Otahuhu. The tidal waters of both oceans wash underneath the traffic, along the southern motorway.

These rivers and the tidal reaches of the Manukau and Waitemata harbours give the regional metropolis an estimated 10 percent of New Zealand's coastline. Much of this was produced when the seas rose around 110 metres after the last ice age, flooding winding river valleys and making islands of the higher ground. Where land meets sea, islands and mudflats provide habitat for masses of migratory birds and extensive sea life.

On land, two substantial mountain ranges define the city edge — the Waitakere Ranges on its western horizon and to the southeast the Hunua Ranges. These provide mountainous preserves rich in plants and wildlife. The city itself sits on a barely dormant volcanic field.

The most recent volcano, Rangitoto Island at the entrance to the Waitemata Harbour, erupted from the seabed less than 600 years ago. There are some 48 volcanoes on the map. These vary in form from the cones of Maungawhau (Mt Eden) and Maungakiekie (One Tree

TAMAKI-MAKAU-RAU

Auckland's Maori name recalls ancient rivalries for possession of this land — it translates as Tamaki of a hundred lovers. The ditches and banks of fortified Maori pa still mark many of the surviving volcanic hills.

Much of the isthmus was burnt and covered in bracken fern when Europeans first settled here in 1840. Maori dug fern root as a food staple.

The coastlines provided fish, shellfish and birds to supplement kumara gardens established in the rich volcanic soil. Old shells in some home gardens still mark places of Maori agriculture in pre-European times. Stone piles and walls where crops were grown may still be traced in farmland around the Manukau Harbour.

◀ *OPPOSITE:* *Summer-flowering pohutukawa grows to the seashore in warmer places in the North Island.*

◀ *PAGES 16–17:* *Maungakiekie (One Tree Hill), one of Auckland's larger volcanoes.*

Hill) to explosion craters now occupied by sea- or freshwater. The Orakei Basin on the edge of central Auckland, and the Onepoto and Tank Farm basins near Takapuna, are all former sites of volcanic activity. Most of the volcanoes date from only 10,000–50,000 years ago. Only five volcanoes are older, and these on a field which began only 150,000 years ago.

While these features are now dressed about with suburbia they provide interesting insights into the geological past, and in some cases enjoyable wild walks, and habitat for birds.

The nature of the Auckland region is also enhanced by its climate; often hot and humid, and largely frost-free. It is here on this isthmus that two major climate zones meet, encouraging an unusually rich range of plants. On the Waitakere Ranges, plants influenced by the subantarctic climates of the south mix with those influenced by the subtropical north. The result is an enriched variety of forest, some 365 native species being recorded.

It is here that many southern plants meet their northern limit while the northern plants approach their southern (largely frost-free) limits. Salt rivers and mudflats here are still lined with substantial mangroves, while kauri, puriri, pohutukawa and a broad range of other northern trees flourish along with the southern hardwoods.

A system of regional parks protects fine examples of this natural world. Many of these parks are located on the coast and attract city dwellers in such numbers that annual visitation rates exceed those of the whole national park system in New

▼ BELOW: *Cliff-girt coasts of the Auckland isthmus are defined by uplifted Waitemata sandstones. The fragile layers are crumbling in many places.*

Zealand. It is still easy to get lost in the larger reserves, however, and a tramping guidebook and survival gear are essential when venturing off the less-beaten tracks of the ranges. Fortunately the regional parks provide fine interepretation services and a plenitude of shorter walks from their convenient carparks.

Small reserves in the suburbs also provide an introduction to the northern forest: the North Shore, for example, has remnant kauri forest at Northcote and Birkenhead; a kahikatea and puriri swamp forest near Takapuna (Smiths Bush); kauri gumfields at Albany; a park where the largely southern hard beech grows with kauri (Le Roys Bush); and coastal forests, such as along the Okura River, fringed with sprawling pohutukawa. (There are several guides to local walks.)

▲ *ABOVE: Smiths Bush, a swamp forest of giant puriri and younger kahikatea, is one of several forest survivors surrounded by suburbs on the North Shore.*

WAITEMATA SANDSTONE

Waitemata sandstone is the name given to the soft, creamy layers of rock that border the shores of the Waitemata Harbour, and elsewhere around the eastern coast. The material was originally laid down in beds of mud under the sea. The eroding cliff faces and foreshores are often spectacularly patterned by layers of sediment distorted by slumping when underwater or by other ancient earth movements. On the outer edge of the Whangaparaoa Peninsula, at Shakespear Regional Park, layers of sandstone are sometimes practically vertical in the reef.

TAKAPUNA FOSSIL FOREST

At the north end of Takapuna Beach on the North Shore lie the fossil remains of an ancient kauri forest. The fossils take the form of tree trunk shapes left behind as basalt lava erupted from nearby Lake Pupuke, perhaps 150,000 years ago. Molten lava from the eruptions flowed over the rim of Pupuke and down to the sea through a stand of forest trees. The trees burned, leaving behind the shape of their stumps, their centres hollow where the trunks burnt out. The fossil forest appears off the Takapuna boat ramp when the tide goes out. There are more stumps and the impressions of fallen branches to be seen in the lava rock northward along the coastal path to Thornes Bay.

▲ *ABOVE:* *Community groups have 'adopted' many local reserves in the city and improved them for nature. In place of a rubbish dump people created this wetland and roosting place for birds, including migrant waders, at Tahuna Torea in the eastern suburbs.*

▶ *RIGHT:* *Takapuna fossil forest.*

MANUKAU HARBOUR

The common image of the Manukau Harbour suffers by comparison with the sparkling Waitemata, yet its forested northern shores and extensive shellbanks are valuable wild habitats. Its very name, meaning place of birds, indicates its importance as a feeding ground for local and migratory wading birds. In summer tens of thousands of waders feed on its mudflats, flying to sandbanks and shorelines as the tide peaks.

Over the decades the Manukau Harbour has served more as a back door to Auckland, less valued as an environment than the Waitemata with its gateway to the Pacific. When an Auckland mayor dissuaded his council from building a sewage works in the shallow waters by Browns Island in the Waitemata, the project was shifted out of sight onto the Manukau. Only recently has the sewage farm around Puketutu Island been dismantled and converted into bird sanctuaries and a recreational coast.

◀ *LEFT: The rock-strewn lava fields on the south side of the Manukau Harbour attracted Maori gardeners and later farmers. The Otuataua Stonefields are on a walkway from Ambury Farm Park, Mangere. The karaka trees appear to be part of a Maori orchard; the stone wall a European construction.*

▲ *ABOVE: Stone walls and Maori stone piles create a warmer microclimate for the growth of subtropical plants like gourds and the sweet potato kumara. Otuataua Stonefields, Manukau.*

AUCKLAND'S CLIMATE

Much of Auckland is largely frost-free, allowing the spread of subtropical mangroves into its rivers, and sustaining the more tender native plants and trees of the north.

Summers are humid, hot and occasionally wet. Winters are frequently wet but generally warmer than places further south. Northerly and westerly winds frequently sweep the city. Conditions can vary from bright sunshine to subtropical downpours then sunshine again, all within one day.

At high tide, the walkway from Ambury Farm Park to the Otuataua Stonefields provides seasonal opportunities to see godwit and knot, South Island pied oystercatcher, wrybill and other plovers, and the hip-high royal spoonbill. Bird counts have recorded thousands of godwit and knot in summer, as well as other species annually migrant from the subarctic regions of Asia and North America.

Standing above the harbour, Mangere Mountain offers fascinating walks through the signs of extensive Maori settlement. The volcanic crater and its rim are marked with distinctive ditches and banks, once topped with palisades, while the sunken pits were once roofed to protect crops of the sweet potato kumara gathered from the rich volcanic soils below.

Further signs of extensive Maori settlement may be traced along the shores of the Manukau, particularly at the Otuataua Stonefields. The stone piles are evidence of the warm shelter these structures provided for the growing of subtropical crops, such as gourds and yams, in pre-European times.

Originally the Manukau was a shallow valley through which, for a period, the Waikato River flowed on its way out to sea. Subsequent volcanic activity round the Bombay Hills blocked that river and shifted its mouth southward. When the last ice age ended, the Tasman Sea filled the

Manukau valley with a shallow harbour covering nearly 400 square kilometres, the second largest in New Zealand.

The northern shore is protected by the bulk of the Waitakere Ranges, where forest regrowth bounds the coastal road from Titirangi through to Whatipu.

The southern shores are extensively farmed, infiltrated by mangrove-lined tidal creeks, and not readily accessible.

The outer edge of the Manukau is part of the huge complex of sandhills built up over the ages as volcanic sands from the central North Island mixed with ironsands swept northward from the Taranaki coast. The Maori 'lost land' of Porae once extended for a kilometre or more off the Manukau South Head but its sandflats and gardens were swept away more than 200 years ago by these coastal currents.

▲ *TOP: South Island pied oystercatchers are 'internal migrants', flocking to the Manukau Harbour between breeding seasons.*

▲ *ABOVE: The rising tide drives birds ashore to rest, here on the edge of suburban Manukau.*

FRANKLIN VOLCANOES

To the south of Auckland, in the Franklin district, another field of some 80 volcanoes dates from half a million to 1.5 million years ago. More eroded than the Auckland volcanoes, they nevertheless can be detected in such landscape features as Pukekohe Hill and the red volcanic earth of the market gardens.

WAITAKERE & WEST COAST

A truly rugged range of volcanic mountains lies on the western horizon of Auckland. Ridges, peaks, broken valleys, rocky bluffs and sheer cliffs form this wild barrier, falling into the Tasman Sea. Much is densely forested, protected by regional parkland.

The Waitakere Ranges were born some 25 million years ago when chains of volcanoes erupted off the west coast of the upper North Island, along with those following a parallel line along the Coromandel Ranges. The mountains were raised from their marine beginnings during the Kaikoura Orogeny, the still-active process which forced up many of New Zealand's mountains some 15 million years ago. Since then erosion has carved them into a steep and twisted range, once densely forested in kauri and other native timber species. Substantial regrowth has seen the ranges largely reclothed since milling days. On the landward side substantial forest, including mature kauri, is preserved in the Cascade Kauri Park. On the seaward side bush gullies and windswept shrub forests clamber over broken heights where original forest remnants may still persist in the face of the timber-millers and pioneer fires.

Despite their proximity to New Zealand's two largest cities, the ranges can be forbidding and dangerous for the tramper. For the motorist, however, there is ready access along the crest of the ranges by way of the Scenic Drive. It is from there that steep and winding roads fall to the isolated settlements along the coast. To get from one bay to another generally involves a winding drive back to the spine of the ranges then a journey down another valley system to reach the next beach.

The regional park headquarters at Arataki on the Scenic Drive gives a fine introduction to the watersheds and nature of the Waitakere Ranges. The views from the information centre show the character of the forested valleys. Loop walks from Arataki explore the nature of the forest, from young shrub growth to a group of established kauri.

The roads down to the coastal settlements are often narrow and winding, made unpleasant when young drivers rush for the surf beaches. The coast makes the effort worthwhile, however. The roads wind through regrowth forest but there are sheltered corners where

◀ OPPOSITE: *Thick coastal rainforest flourishes near the west coast of the Waitakere Ranges. Frequent rain, and here a tiny overhead waterfall, keeps a corner of the Forest and Bird Matuku Reserve rich in species.*

▲ *ABOVE: The wild west coast has dangerous seas which can unexpectedly sweep over its rock platforms. The ever-changing tidal currents can also suck swimmers out to sea in moments. Keep a careful eye on the sea when clambering on rocks, especially when the tides are up: swim only on patrolled beaches, and then only between the surf-club flags.*

pohutukawa and forest trees overlie the exotic-looking nikau palms and masses of coastal forest shrubs such as kawakawa, whau, kanuka, manuka and flax.

Whatipu at the southern end is accessed from the Scenic Drive near Titirangi and overlooks the wild entry to the Manukau Harbour. The road twists out there along the Manukau shores then clambers over a saddle to reveal the expansive black sandflats. The shifting sands of the Manukau Bar claimed many vessels in the days when sailing ships approached Auckland by this route: in 1863 HMS *Orpheus* struck and foundered here with the loss of 189 men.

Loads of timber milled from the valleys along the coast were once brought here by steam tramway to be loaded onto sailing ships sheltering against the black bulk of Paratutai at the harbour mouth. The railway line can still be traced in places where foundation piles rise above the moving sands.

The extensive fields of black sand originate from volcanic activity down the Taranaki coast, and from inland by way of the Waikato River, the sand carried here by long shore currents.

The present sandflats are very young, having built up between the mid-1930s and mid-1950s. Covering 820 hectares they constitute the Whatipu Sands Scientific Reserve, an area of dunes and wetlands extending 7 kilometres north along the coast. The golden sand-dune binder pingao is spreading here along with rush and other wetland communities.

The flats are visited by a good range of wetland birds. Both New Zealand and banded dotterel occur, sharing the sand-

flats with migrant waders such as godwit and knot in summer. Walks beneath vast cliffs pass a huge sea cave on a route along the sandflats as far as Karekare. To reach this next settlement by road, however, involves a return to the Scenic Drive and a turn-off at the Waiatarua radio masts. The Waiatarua turn-off serves three beach settlements, each approached by its own branch road.

Karekare is a popular surf beach, reached from the carpark by walking over the dunes. It too was once the scene of timber-milling, connected to Whatipu by the steam tramway round the coast. The bulk of the Watchman, in the middle of the beach, is the remains of an eroding volcanic dome. Just offshore, Panatahi Island is used by young male seals as a haul-out, while red-billed gulls and white-fronted terns nest there.

▲ *ABOVE: The Whatipu sands lie just outside the entrance to Manukau Harbour. The steep rock of Paratutai at the entrance once sheltered a wharf where kauri timber was loaded for export.*

▲ ABOVE: *Colourful fruit of the nikau palm which flourishes in warm corners of the Waitakere forest. The slow-growing tree is the southernmost of palm species.*

Next north is Piha, also once connected by the spectacular timber railway but now approached by its own branch road. The bulk of volcanic Lion Rock divides the surf beach in two. North along the coast is Anawhata.

This whole coast is marked with a complex of volcanic features which give it a spectacular visual apeal. The many caves and defensible high points were important living places for Maori in pre-European times.

In many places, milling and fires have affected the forest cover, much of which is a mass of windswept regrowth, a protective mat of shrub species running back from the sea cliffs.

Bethells or Te Henga is another black sand beach with interesting natural features. Its windswept dunes have marched inland to contain Lake Wainamu, home of wetland birds. On the coastal headland of Erangi Point is a colony of spotted shags; grey-faced petrels, protected by the steep cliffs, nest in burrows on the islands just offshore.

On the way to Te Henga the road passes an extensive wetland of 80 hectares known as Bethells Swamp. Direct access to Forest and Bird's Matuku wetland reserve is available from the other shore by following Jonkers Road and walking down through the forest to the water. The clogged course of the Waitakere River is rich habitat, including among its birds the bittern, fernbird, banded rail and crake.

The Cascade Kauri Park and Auckland City Walk lie further upstream, accessible through the Waitakere Golf Course off Falls Road, 2 kilometres from Te Henga Road. Here mature kauri is preserved,

marching along a ridge fronted with rimu, kahikatea, tanekaha and large puriri. The easy and circular Auckland City Walk exposes the nature of the northern forest with giant trees and an understorey of kowhai, tree ferns, vines and clambering plants. The forest birdlife includes a colony of sulphur-crested cockatoo, while long-tailed bats have been recorded along the river.

In an 1100 hectare area of Cascade Kauri Park, Forest and Bird and local government have introduced a project called Ark in the Park. Intensive pest control has allowed native birds to flourish and others to be reintroduced: among them are saddleback/tieke, North Island robin, whitehead and kokako.

At the northern end of the Waitakere Ranges, Muriwai is approached over open country from Waimauku on the Auckland–Helensville SH16. Here are the last of the

▲ *ABOVE: From Muriwai Regional Park, an ocean beach sweeps around 50 kilometres northward to South Kaipara Head. The sandhills surround coastal dune lakes and protect the Kaipara Harbour from the Tasman Sea.*

giant cliffs and rocky reefs. From here the lonely dunes and black-sand beaches run north to the mouth of the Kaipara Harbour, 50 kilometres away.

Besides having its own gannet colony Oaia Island, a kilometre offshore, is a haul-out area for New Zealand fur seals, which sometimes come close to the mainland shore. Gannets which nest on the top of the Motutara rock stack, just off the mainland, share their eyrie with white-fronted terns which nest about the side of the rock.

Access to the gannet colonies is a short walk out from the Maori Bay carpark or

GANNETS AT MURIWAI

The mainland gannet colonies at Muriwai are a relatively recent phenomenon. The birds originally established their colonies on Oaia Island off the coast but overflow populations onto Motutara, a rock stack just offshore, soon spread to the mainland cliffs. Fences established in the early 1980s protect the birds from predators and dogs and have encouraged more and more gannets to breed there. One reason for the burgeoning population is that young gannets migrate in their first season to southern and eastern Australian waters but return after three to seven years to breed in the place of their birth. Nests are established from late July with the peak of nesting activity in November. The colony is vacated in late autumn and winter.

▶ *OPPOSITE, TOP: The gannet colonies of Muriwai originated on Oaia Island, a kilometre from the mainland, which is also a resting place for New Zealand fur seals. Next they occupied Motutara rock stack just offshore, an islet named for the white-fronted terns which nest in its flanks. Gannets spilled over onto the mainland in 1979 and viewing platforms and fences were soon built to protect the colonies. A million people visit the regional park each year.*

▶ *OPPOSITE, BOTTOM LEFT AND RIGHT: Visitor paths and fences built in the early 1980s protect the mainland gannet colonies at Muriwai from predators. This has encouraged more and more gannets to breed on the cliff tops. One reason for the burgeoning population is that young gannets migrate in their first season to southern and eastern Australian waters then return after three to seven years to breed in the place where they hatched.*

a walk up the headland from Muriwai Beach. In the cliffs behind the carpark is a geologically famous exposure of lava pillows. These appear as round cross sections of the lava tubes, exuded like toothpaste during an underwater eruption and subsequently lifted with the formation of the ranges.

Muriwai Beach has been built up by the northward drift of volcanic sand. It forms the outer edge of the giant, unstable sand bar which encloses the Kaipara Harbour. Extensive pine forests were planted from the 1930s to halt the landward drift of the sand, isolating a series of dune lakes where rare dabchicks, fernbird, bittern and other wetland species once thrived.

Muriwai Beach runs for 50 kilometres to South Kaipara Head. A walk along the beach will reveal the little white skeleton coils of the ram's horn or spirula, a squid-like creature which floats after its prey in the ocean depths. The violet snail also floats in the Tasman Sea, feeding on jellyfish. Bivalve shells buried in the sand include the hand-sized toheroa, a meaty shellfish, now absolutely protected after decades of over-harvesting.

Look for New Zealand dotterel and banded dotterel, along with variable oystercatcher and terns, which may nest at midsummer just above the high tide line. Where the beach curves round South Kaipara Head to form Papakanui Spit, Caspian and white-fronted terns nest along with gulls, dotterels, and perhaps one or two pairs of the endangered fairy tern in summer. Such birds are always at risk from off-road vehicles driven (legally) up the beach.

AUCKLAND'S REGIONAL PARKS

Auckland's system of regional parklands is the envy of other communities. It was begun in the 1960s by an inspirational group of regional councillors who saw the need for the gradual acquisition of natural 'lungs' for the growing city.

The original parks included landmark coastal properties, some of which combined farming with recreational use. Many of the later acquisitions include extensive natural areas. A strong conservation ethic now drives management. Volunteer work parties help with pest control and reafforestation in many blocks. For example, Tawharanui Peninsula has been protected with a pest-exclusion fence and kiwi introduced. Pest control has led to the reintroduction of birds such as the bush robin to parks at Wenderholm and in the Waitakere Ranges.

The Auckland regional parks extend down the eastern coast from Rodney district southward to the Firth of Thames. In the west there are protected areas from the Kaipara Harbour to the Awhitu Peninsula on the south head of the Manukau Harbour. Auckland City's Centennial Park in the Waitakere Ranges is now part of the regional park system and the centre of habitat recovery work by Forest and Bird and the regional council.

In 2010, the regional park system totalled more than 40,000 hectares in 26 parks with at least three more due for development or expansion. It gives public access to more than 100 kilometres of coast and 500 kilometres of tramping tracks. Entry to the parks is free.

The regional park system is visited more than eight million times a year, around twice the sum total of visits to all of New Zealand's national parks put together. There are comparatively few parks of the kind operated by the Department of Conservation in other regions. DoC's land management is extensive on the offshore islands of the Hauraki Gulf, however.

▶ *OPPOSITE TOP: Tawharanui Regional Park occupies an extensive peninsula, northeast of Warkworth. A pest-excluding fence at the isthmus makes it safe for introduced kiwi and petrel colonies.*

▶ *OPPOSITE, MIDDLE: Duder Regional Park is a former farm on the edge of the Firth of Thames.*

▶ *OPPOSITE, BOTTOM: Wenderholm Regional Park is on the coast road north of the city. Reintroduced bush robin breed in the cliff-top forest.*

◀ *LEFT: The Auckland City Walk, a one-hour loop in the Cascade Kauri Park. Kowhai flowers golden in spring.*

THE HAURAKI GULF

The passing of the ice ages did much to shape the sheltered waters of the Hauraki Gulf. Open country and forests which once sloped eastward toward the Coromandel Peninsula drowned in the rising waters. About 6500 years ago, the rising sea level rode up the sinuous rivers and made islands of many hills and promontories.

Auckland's east coast is now deeply penetrated by the sea, with fingers of peninsula land providing extensive coastlines, and sheltering long bays and estuaries. The regional parks which string along the coast from Long Bay on the urban fringe to Tawharanui Peninsula 70 kilometres to the north preserve magnificent beaches and spectacular remnants of the old pohutukawa and coastal forest. Visit the parks for long walks on the edges of the Hauraki Gulf; enjoy the trees of the coastal forest, the sandstone and basalt reefs, and the vision of passing sea- and shorebirds. Whales and dolphins are sometimes seen, along with flocks of shearwaters and petrels, some 12 species of which nest on the islands and rock stacks of the gulf.

The Hauraki Gulf contains more than a hundred named islands and islets, most of them protected by the Department of Conservation, and some the home of New Zealand's rarest species of birds and lizards. Public access to these islands is limited but there are regular ferry services to two with significant natural features: the young volcano of Rangitoto, and Tiritiri Matangi Island with its open bird sanctuary. Watch for seabirds on the way, particularly in summer when migratory species return to breed.

▲ *ABOVE: At high summer the pohutukawa flowers on the islands of the Hauraki Gulf.*

◀ *OPPOSITE: On Tiritiri Matangi Island, the summer flax flowers are an important source of nectar for honeyeaters.*

RANGITOTO
THE YOUNGEST VOLCANO

The gentle cone of Rangitoto Island (2311 hectares) sits like an upturned saucer off the entrance to Auckland Harbour. While it is the defining landmark of the city, visible from many shores, Rangitoto is probably only 600 years old. An archaeological investigation on adjacent Motutapu Island revealed footprints in old Maori gardens buried by the volcano's ash.

Accessed by ferry from downtown Auckland, the island is still building its plant cover over raw blocks of scoria and basalt reefs. The bare rock fields are stove hot in summer, barely stained with primitive algae. There is virtually no soil so plants rely on a humus built up from dead leaves and bird droppings. What plants there are grow in the shade

▲ *TOP: The cone of Rangitoto appears the same shape from many North Shore beaches.*

◀ *LEFT, TOP TO BOTTOM: The pohutukawa forests of Rangitoto bloom just prior to Christmas. The surface of the island is covered in raw scoria and basalt blocks from which a forest of pohutukawa is gradually growing. Delicate plants grow in their shade, including green bush orchid (left) and clambering native clematis (right).*

of a spreading forest of pohutukawa, many a local hybrid with northern rata. These trees draw their sustenance from a meniscus of water lying many metres below. They shelter quite delicate plants including orchids, particularly in spring, and the kidney fern, which dries like a potato chip then flourishes green again with the rain.

In spring thousands of black-backed gulls nest on the scoria flats about a kilometre west from the Rangitoto wharf building. Another track leads 4 kilometres to the summit at 259 metres. The apparent knobs, obvious from the mainland and likened by Maori to the 'knuckles of the chief Peretu', emerge as older cones ringing the central crater. There are further tracks, including one round the coast to Islington Bay and the causeway that leads to Motutapu Island. Motutapu consists of rolling farmland, though long-term reafforestation progammes are underway. In the past both islands suffered from tree damage by possums and wallabies, which were exterminated in the 1990s.

MAORI NAMES

Rangitoto and Motutapu are ancient names which occur elsewhere in Polynesia and within New Zealand. Rangitoto is generally regarded as referring to the day of the 'bleeding of Tama Te Kapua', captain of the migration canoe Te Arawa, who cut himself on the sharp rocks (Te rangi totongia a Tama te Kapua), or simply to an island of 'bloody skies' which it must have seemed to those who observed the fire-fountaining eruption. Motutapu is simply 'sacred island'.

The rocky nature of Rangitoto calls for strong footwear to protect the feet, though there is a tractor trip available to near the summit. Be sure to take drinking water; there is none on the island.

TIRITIRI MATANGI
THE OPEN SANCTUARY

Tiritiri Matangi Island Open Sanctuary provides an opportunity for visitors to see some of the rarest birds in New Zealand. In the past 20 years it has been developed as a showcase island for nature, a living demonstration of what community conservation can achieve. After more than a century of farming only scraps of forest remained in its gullies, while the flat-topped island was choked with old pastures. Yet red-crowned parakeet persisted as did the little black spotless crake and the bellbird, extinct on the adjacent mainland.

▲ *ABOVE: This sheltered bay on Tiritiri Matangi Island is a popular anchorage. The island is open for visitors to enjoy its free-living rare birds (and tuatara) which have been progressively introduced as trees and ponds have been established. Thousands of community volunteers, conservationists and schools helped in the replanting of a grazing farm.*

When the guardian Tiri lighthouse was automated in 1984 the lighthouse-keeper stayed on to supervise the reafforestation of the island.

Community, school and conservation groups took turns to plant out food trees for native birds. The Pacific rat, which in summer reached a population of 250 a hectare, was eradicated, creating safer conditions for nesting birds, lizards and insects.

Populations of burrow-nesting grey-faced petrels grew in the shelter of the shrubs. Tuatara were introduced.

Feeding stations and nesting boxes were built to supplement the food sources and nesting shelter because the island lacked enough of the mature trees some birds require. Then the introductions were made: whitehead, saddleback, stitchbird and robin, rifleman, little spotted kiwi, brown teal, kokako, and some hand-reared takahe which promptly bred. The rapidly expanding population of some birds, such as the robin, has led to their capture and release in other reserves.

Tiritiri Matangi Island (218 hectares) is about 4 kilometres off the Whangaparaoa Peninsula. Access is by ferry from Auckland, or a shorter voyage from Gulf Harbour near the end of the peninsula. After a briefing from duty staff visitors can spend the day wandering the island paths and meeting near-tame wild birds close up. The open-sanctuary concept, using volunteer workers, is a way of gaining public support for conservation while easing pressure on the absolute sanctuaries of the farther gulf islands.

▲ TOP: *The Tiritiri lighthouse, once one of the most powerful in the world, is now automatic but still a focus for visitors who picnic there.*

▲ ABOVE: *One of the world's rarest birds, the notornis or takahe was rediscovered in a remote Fiordland valley in 1948 after 50 years. Several takahe now live and nest successfully on Tiritiri Matangi.*

KAWAU
GOVERNOR GREY'S PRIVATE ZOO

Kawau (25,000 hectares) lies in the mouth of the broad Matakana river system, a ferry ride from Sandspit near Warkworth (or much longer from Auckland, cruising past the inner islands of the gulf). It is notable as the home of an early governor and later premier, Sir George Grey, who introduced a bizarre range of animals from around the world in the 1860s. He had zebra to draw his carriage, monkeys, antelope, kangaroos and wallabies. Kawau was the site of earlier copper mining and a Cornish pumphouse on the coast attracts visitors. Ferries land at Mansion House Bay where the governor expanded the early mine manager's house, now open to the public.

The island still has wallabies introduced by Grey: the Parma or white-throated wallaby, virtually extinct in its native South Australia, was rediscovered among the five species he introduced, and exported back to its homeland in the 1980s. His garden includes Chilean oil palms and sprawling Moreton Bay figs.

Interesting birds include the ground-dwelling weka, the reintroduced brown kiwi and the occasional kookaburra, a small population of which has spread to the quieter corners of the adjacent mainland. Kawau is named for the shag or cormorant, colonies of which occupy trees which overhang the sea in places.

The despoliation by both wallabies and the brush-tailed possum has had an extraordinary effect on the island. A few pohutukawa survive from once extensive coastal forests but the major tree cover is now kanuka and manuka. By 1971, the introduced pests had eradicated all but six native plant species in the vicinity of Mansion House. Efforts are now made to control these pests.

Kawau is largely in private hands but a mailboat cruise of its sheltered bays gives a flavour of the island, and glimpses of dolphins and seabirds which abound in these waters. Mansion House is publicly owned and there are interesting walks in its vicinity, including to the remains of the Cornish-style coppermine pumphouse.

▲ *TOP: An early governor and later premier, Sir George Grey, bought the mine-manager's house on Kawau Island and created his own private world.*

▲ *ABOVE: The mine pumphouse from the 1840s is a landmark of Kawau Island.*

GOAT ISLAND
THE PIONEERING MARINE RESERVE

Cape Rodney near Leigh marks the landward end of the Hauraki Gulf. An 800-metre-wide coastal swathe protects the waters from here to Okakari Point in New Zealand's first marine reserve, created in 1975.

The marine reserve is popularly known as Goat Island, a reference to the island which lies only 138 metres offshore. Shoals of blue maomao, parore and snapper can be seen in the shallow water. Snorkellers and divers enjoy the sight of goatfish and trevally, along with eagle rays lying on the sand. The reefs are home to a further range of fish, and red crayfish which have practically disappeared from the unprotected coasts nearby. A glass-bottomed boat tour circumnavigates the island. The seas are studied by students and researchers from the University of Auckland's Marine Research Laboratory on the clifftop.

Stretching north from the bulk of the coastal hills, beyond Goat Island, are the white-sand beaches and dunelands of Pakiri. Along its 14 kilometres stretch, the endangered New Zealand dotterel and variable oystercatcher breed in summer. Similar coastline then runs north from Te Arai to Mangawhai South Head where Caspian terns and sometimes fairy terns nest below the giant dunes. Motor access to these beaches is limited to occasional forest tracks, and there are walks at Te Arai Point.

The coast of the Long Bay Regional Park on the northern edge of Auckland is also protected in a marine reserve, but there is nothing in particular to see. The Pollen Island Marine Reserve, beside the northwestern motorway in Auckland, is a combination of mudflat, shellbank and mangroves protecting an endemic moth and the shorebirds which shelter and nest there. Access is difficult and visits are not encouraged because of the fragile habitat. A marine protected area (under different legislation) just off the Tawharanui beaches, beyond Warkworth, makes for interesting snorkelling and diving around the mid-beach promontory.

GREAT BARRIER ISLAND

Following the line of the Coromandel Ranges and Mt Moehau 20 kilometres out to sea is another remnant of the old ranges, named Great Barrier Island by James Cook. Similar in geography to the Coromandel Range, its landscape comprises a series of deeply eroded volcanic stumps, among them Mt Hobson/ Hirakimata, rising to 621 metres. The

▲ *ABOVE: Goat Island Beach just north of Leigh draws thousands of visitors, particularly in summer, to see the shoals of blue maomao, snapper and parore massed in the shallows. These waters were protected in New Zealand's first marine reserve in 1975.*

sinuous and mainly rocky coast is backed in places by wetlands frequented by many birds.

The island is 40 kilometres long but its harbours intrude so far inland that its maximum width is only 15 kilometres. Much of its mountain landscape in the north is clothed in rainforest but the original kauri have been felled throughout the island and great expanses of kanuka and manuka scrubland have taken over.

Wetlands are retained and shelter several duck species, as well as fernbirds.

The island is free of mustelids — ferrets, stoats and weasels — while possums, Norway rats and hedgehogs are also absent. Consequently the birdlife is rich and varied.

Notable wildlife includes a widespread population of brown teal, now largely gone from the mainland. Kaka, the forest parrot, is still seen in flocks, with young males wandering in spring as far as the mainland to feed on blossom such as kowhai. The threatened black petrel nests among the peaks in early summer. The banded rail is seen by the road.

While Great Barrier is New Zealand's fourth largest island it is sparsely settled:

▲ *TOP: The rugged pinnacles on the spine of Great Barrier Island. This was the scene of early mining and kauri-timber felling.*

▲ *ABOVE: Harbour arms penetrate the land, protecting beaches and wetlands.*

by farmers, fisher folk, alternative life-stylers and increasingly those providing for the tourist trade. While there is a basic roading system on the island most visitors fly there and hire transport.

THE SEABIRD COAST

The mudflats and shellbanks of the Firth of Thames are host to literally thousands of wading birds which nest in the Arctic tundra and fly 15,000 kilometres to spend the summer here. Wading birds which breed in southern New Zealand also flock to the Firth to recover in season.

The Firth of Thames is the southern end of the Hauraki Gulf, a down-faulted block lying between the bulk of the Hunua Ranges, southwest of Auckland, and the Coromandel Peninsula (page 74). Its shallow shores are widely protected under the Ramsar Convention as a wetland of international importance.

While flocks of godwit and knot migrate to several of New Zealand's shallow harbours and estuaries, this is the place with the greatest population. As the tide rises the birds are driven off their feeding grounds over the mudflats to roost along the shore. The sight of masses of birds flying in close-knit flocks is one of the great natural experiences of birdwatching in New Zealand.

The Miranda Shorebird Centre is the focus for enthusiasts and visitors, with an information centre, volunteer guides, some basic accommodation and observation hides. Access is off the Hauraki Plains highway or over the shoulder of the Hunua Ranges and down the coast of the Firth. The winding coastal road passes through attractive forest reserves, passing regional parks which link the shingle shores with the inland ranges. The Hunua Ranges were thrust up in the same movements which created the Waitakere Ranges and are similarly rugged. They are mostly enjoyed by trampers, but a population of kokako is being built up following intensive pest control. Near Miranda, hot springs at the foot of the hills are a reminder of activity below.

The Arctic waders arrive on the Firth of Thames in October in the New Zealand spring, as lean grey-coloured birds. As autumn approaches their russet breeding dress emerges and the birds fly back to the northern hemisphere in late March–April. Non-breeding birds can be seen through the winter, however.

The bar-tailed godwit come mostly from Alaska and northeast Siberia; its half-sized companion, the eastern knot, breeds in northern Asia. Among these major migrants are smaller numbers of other Arctic waders including turnstone, red-necked stint, golden plover, various sandpipers and the eastern curlew, standing head and shoulders above other roosting birds. Altogether some

◀ *OPPOSITE: Godwits and knots gather on a shell bank at Miranda, Firth of Thames as the tide rises. (The eastern knot is the smaller bird.) Both are summer migrants from the subarctic. White-fronted terns fly beyond.*

▲ ABOVE: As migration time approaches birds gather in swirling masses, when the tide drives them close to shore.

39 different waders from the northern hemisphere have been recorded here (some only once) but regular visitors include bar-tailed godwit and eastern knot by the thousands, ruddy turnstone, eastern curlew, sharp-tailed sandpiper, terek sandpiper, red-necked stint and curlew sandpiper.

The Firth of Thames attracts internal migrants too: almost half the national population of the endangered wrybill plover (with its beak twisting to the right) feed on the mudflats from December/ January till August. Then they fly back to the shingle riverbeds of the South Island high country where they breed.

MIGRANT BIRDS

New Zealand is the summer feeding place for tens of thousands of wading birds which make an incredible journey each year from their subarctic breeding grounds. The godwit and the knot are the best known for they can be easily seen on tidal mudflats and estuaries in flocks of hundreds from spring till autumn. Others subarctic waders include various plovers and dotterels, snipe, sandpipers, whimbrels and curlews, and the sparrow-sized red-necked stint.

During the past 25 years, the New Zealand Wader Study Group has banded the legs of around 20,000 birds captured in nets over the northern mudflats. Observations of the leg tags seen along the course of the Asian Flyway, and more recently satellite tracking, has helped establish their migratory routes and flight times.

Studies have found most of the bar-tailed godwit originate from breeding grounds in the North American tundra, not Asia. By the shortest route that is 12,000 kilometres round the curve of the earth, but observations suggest the birds follow the coasts of Asia, making their migration a journey of 15,000 kilometres.

It is thought the godwit fly continuously to reach New Zealand for few are seen resting on the way. Going back north the birds take more time, for mid-March is far too early to nest in the frozen tundra. Godwit first fly to China, Korea and Japan, probably non-stop, a journey of 8500 kilometres. They then spend a month on the east Asia coast before making a final flight to Alaska.

There is argument about how they navigate. Theories have included following the stars, or lines of magnetic force emanating from the Earth. Modern theories include some allowance for following major land features and sea coasts, inferring an inherited knowledge of geography.

Young birds just hatched in the tundra fly to New Zealand later than their parents. Nevertheless, these young birds tend to spend the New Zealand summers in the same harbours as their parents or nearby. Some thousands of these young birds spend the following winter here before migrating the next season.

▲ TOP: The rare wrybill plover, a bird peculiar
New Zealand, is an 'internal migrant'. It breeds on
braided riverbeds in the South Island then migrates
to northern estuaries.

▲ ABOVE: The kotuku or white heron is a rare visitor
at several harbours in summer and autumn.

◀ LEFT: Members of the New Zealand Wader Study
Group band bar-tailed godwit as part of their research
into migration to the subarctic. Experiments using
tiny radio transmitters and satellites have defined the
extraordinary journeys of these birds.

NORTHLAND

NORTHLAND

The physical feel of changing nature begins in the northern suburbs of Auckland and deepens as the road heads north. This is the country where frosts are few and the tails of cyclones lash in from the tropics several times a year. Warm, wet and lush, Northland is popularly known as 'the winterless north', an exaggeration perhaps but the subtropical influence has a profound effect on its nature and wildlife.

The region has a number of tree species which need the frost-free climate, each with its own associated plants and animals. Some trees, widespread in the forests south of Auckland, are replaced here by local relatives. Other trees, like the ancient rimu and kahikatea, grow here and throughout the country.

Most spectacular of the 'locals' is the giant kauri, basis of the timber and gum-mining industries for a century and a half. The aesthetic effect of the Christmas-flowering pohutukawa, which prefers warm coasts, is another memorable feature. Mangroves grow larger and are more widespread in the north.

The maritime environment is generous, with sheltering headlands, golden beaches, rough rock reefs and clusters of islands offshore.

The roads north from the Auckland isthmus are two-fold, advertised on touring signs as the Twin Coast Discovery Highway, and providing the opportunity to make a round trip of the great peninsula. Many of the most memorable places are on side roads off SH1, on the east coast, and not directly connected to each other. Take a detailed map, prepare to drive on gravel roads, and explore off the main road.

FINDING THE WAY

State Highway 16 skirts the southern Kaipara Harbour to Wellsford before joining SH1, which runs up the eastern side of the island. The road branches again at Brynderwyn, with SH1 crossing the mountains to Whangarei and beyond.

The alternative route, SH12 around the northwestern Kaipara, ultimately follows the west coast — the kauri coast — to the Waipoua kauri forests and Hokianga.

◀ OPPOSITE: Looking across the entrance to Hokianga Harbour, on the west coast of Northland. The waterway extends inland some 30 kilometres, touching on early Maori settlements, trading posts and missions from the early nineteenth century. The sand dunes rise to 170 metres.

◀ PAGES 50–51: Kanuka trees fringe a typical west-coast dune lake on South Kaipara Head, lower Northland.

KAIPARA &
THE KAURI COAST

The Kaipara Harbour is reputedly one of the largest in the world, but it is shallow and dangerous to enter. The harbour is held in by two long tombolos of sand, both serviced by country roads. The South Head road runs 50 kilometres north of Muriwai, a strip of huge sandhills, plantation forests and a few dune lakes (see pages 33–34). The North Head road runs 74 kilometres south from Dargaville to the Pouto settlement.

The entry to the Kaipara Harbour is 7 kilometres wide, taken up by wild water and shifting sandbanks which wrecked many ships during the kauri export days of the nineteenth century.

Altogether the Kaipara coastline of open harbour and drowned river valleys totals 3200 kilometres. In the south its contributing rivers flow from the vicinity of Auckland. Its northern tributaries rise in swampland, northwest of Whangarei, nearly on the other side of the island. The once busy sailing route between Helensville, near Auckland, and Dargaville in the north is 65 kilometres long.

The Kaipara Harbour formed as the last ice age ended, raising sea levels and flooding the coastal river valleys of Northland. The subsequent longshore drift of sand gave the harbour its outside edge, its west coast. The harbour's shallow waters include many sandbanks and mudflats, making it a fine habitat for wading birds and seabirds. Threatened and endangered New Zealand birds, such as the New Zealand dotterel and variable oystercatcher, are joined in summer by thousands of birds from the Arctic tundra. One of the rarest is a New Zealand population of fairy tern, with around 13 pairs, some of which breed on the South Kaipara Head on the Papakanui Spit (page 34).

The shallow harbour, silted by the removal of forest trees, is lined in many places with mangroves. The largest overhang the tidal streams — where the flowing water carries the most nutrients — while those behind assemble back to the highest tide marks.

Taking SH12 west from Brynderwyn gives the best view of the Kaipara and its character. Long harbour arms reach through the low hills towards the highway where side roads give access to the old milling and gum towns. Most are

◀ *OPPOSITE: Northland's special tree, the kauri, distinguished by its clear trunk, making it a target of nineteenth-century timber millers.*

▲ *ABOVE: A tidal river near Matakohe lined with mangroves. Their breathing tubes can be seen rising through the mud in the foreground.*

▲ *TOP: Occasional patches of coastal forest survive on the sandhills which separate the Kaipara Harbour from the Tasman Sea. Parallel lines on the farther hill are the remains of the ditch and bank defences of an early Maori pa or fortress.*

FORESTS IN THE SEA

Mangroves grow in saltwater, their roots drowned twice a day by high tide.

The trees have broad-spreading roots equipped with upright breathing pegs which rise above the mud. Their leaves also sweat excess salt.

Frost-sensitive, they grow largest — up to 5 metres — farthest north. About their southern limit (around Kawhia) the trees are little more than ankle height and their place in saltwater creeks and harbours is then taken by rushes.

BIRDWATCHING

Tapora, opposite the harbour entrance, is a favourite spot for birdwatching. Birds gather on Big Sand Island before high tide. (Access across private land.)

just holiday settlements now, unlike the nineteenth century when kauri timber was felled and milled here. Mills whined all day, while coastal and foreign-going ships loaded cargoes of timber and kauri gum. The atmosphere of this past is best caught at the magnificent Kauri Museum on a short side-loop at Matakohe.

The road then continues around the extensive flats that stretch beside the Wairoa River arm of the harbour. The Ruawai flats and beyond are farmed for dairying and the sweet potato, known in New Zealand as kumara, a staple root crop.

Ferries once crossed this broad tidal waterway to formerly important local centres such as Te Kopuru, practically a ghost town now, where sailing ships were built of kauri and exports loaded.

Where the road and river round a bluff there is a steep cone rising from the low hills. Tokatoka is the remnant plug of an ancient volcano.

The old port of Dargaville was once a centre of the timber-milling industry. Now it straggles along the riverfront, the gateway down to Kaipara North Head and Pouto on the one hand, and the kauri forests to the north.

The journey north from Dargaville follows roughly the line of an abandoned railway which once took out the kauri logs from the interior. The damp valley and the rising inland slopes of Tutamoe are marked by plantations of exotic pine forests.

It is not until the approach to the Waipoua Forest that the land begins to reflect its early riches. Scientifically, kauri is classified as *Agathis australis*. It is a conifer, evolved before the formation of flowering plants. As such it is related to similar giant species in Australia, the western Pacific and Malaysia.

THE KAURI MUSEUM

The Kauri Museum is by any standards an outstanding museum of regional life. It develops the theme of the kauri tree and its related industries which have transformed the north over the past 200 years. A million hectares of kauri-dominated forests once clothed northern New Zealand. Spars and masts for European naval vessels were first taken in the late eighteenth century; related industries such as kauri-gum digging, milling and shipbuilding followed.

The museum combines life-sized relics of the technology of timber exploitation, but also shows the people of the time, modelled in settings as varied as bush huts and pioneer buildings, a life-sized boarding house and sawmill, and the interiors of grand houses, with their art and pioneer furnishings.

Major collections of the gum (or copal) show the natural beauty exposed, and showcase the ornamentation produced by gumdiggers. The technology of gum digging and its export for the manufacture of varnish and linoleum is also displayed. (See gum digging, page 69.)

▲ *ABOVE: Stationary steam engine and timber winch, one of the exterior exhibits at The Kauri Museum at Matakohe.*

An easy place to enjoy the kauri forests is just off SH12 in a low valley a little distance to the east of the main road. This began as a private reserve of 25 hectares donated to the government in 1915 by James Trounson, for whom it is named. Now expanded to 425 hectares, it has easy walks through a concentration of kauri trees. Trounson Reserve is also distinguished as an early 'mainland island' where intensive pest control is used to help preserve threatened birds such as kiwi.

Nearby, the forest lookout off SH12 provides a view over the ridges of the Waipoua Forest (9105 hectares), in turn joined to the Matarau and Waima forests further inland. Many kauri are concentrated up the ridges, their spreading crowns growing in feathery-looking patches above the surrounding forest.

They also grow along the roadside, sheer straight trunks, like grey barrels, lifting huge branched crowns.

Kauri is generally part of a mixed rainforest, growing with other trees including the giant podocarp pines. Kauri usually grows in patches but with an open understorey of 'kauri grass', an astelia lily and the cutty-grass ghania. The trunks of the mature tree are bare of branches, and of parasitic growths because the bark keeps flaking off. Accumulated leaf falls, a metre and more high, form a heap around the tree, protecting its vulnerable surface roots.

Short off-road walks lead to the most spectacular trees in Waipoua: Tane Mahuta (god of the forest) and Te Matua Ngahere (father of the forest). Both trees have been estimated at between 1800 and 2000 years old. There is enough timber in each to build five or six houses.

From Waipoua, the road descends to the peaceful-looking Hokianga Harbour. This narrow band of tidal water penetrates the land for 30 kilometres inland, a drowned river system nevertheless navigable by pioneer vessels.

Golden sandhills rise up to 170 metres on the northern heads. They overlook the narrow entrance where the Polynesian navigator Kupe is said to have farewelled the land of Aotearoa before returning to his home in Polynesia (Te Hokianga a Kupe).

The harbour has always been a maritime highway between Maori settlements and later trading and timber towns. Tall hills line it on both sides with rolling farmland overlooked by dense forests. These are some of the remnants of the kauri forests,

▲ *ABOVE: Kauri snails, a feature of the damp forest floors where kauri trees grow. They grow to about 5 cm across.*

▶ *OPPOSITE, TOP: Farming has succeeded kauri-timber milling and gumdigging around the shores of the Kaipara Harbour. Rising sea levels after the ice ages drowned several river systems to form the shallow harbour.*

▶ *OPPOSITE, BOTTOM: Sunlight filters through the forest beside the Waipoua River in the kauri sanctuary. Other species grow among the kauri.*

KING OF TREES

The giant kauri tree is regarded as the king among New Zealand trees. Huge forests of kauri once clothed northern New Zealand from south of Auckland and the Coromandel Peninsula.

Originally kauri-dominated forests covered a million hectares of northern New Zealand but now only 7455 hectares of mature forest remains. Kauri is a widespread tree in regenerating forests, however.

Kauri have side branches when young but shed these after 100–120 years. These young kauri trees are known as 'rickers' after their use in rigging ships in the nineteenth century. The bare, straight trunks of a mature kauri produce fine, easily worked softwood.

Kauri trees also leak copal, a gum-like amber, which was the basis of a major export industry from the 1880s to the 1910s. Gum was gathered or dug from the old forest lands, and exported for making high-quality varnish and linoleum (page 69).

standing like islands above the valleys of settlement.

It is possible to cross the long harbour by car ferry from Rawene. Kohukohu on the northern shore is a fine survivor of the great timber-felling and shipping days with pioneer wooden buildings. It is possible to drive further north along remote roads, round small western harbours, and through farms and forests to Kaitaia, capital of the Far North.

Most drivers follow the harbour inland as far as they can on SH12, to Kaikohe and on to Ohaeawai and the junction with SH1. This is a faster trip through Northland's mixed rainforest, and a direct inland route to Kaitaia over the Maungataniwha Range. Alternatively it is possible to wander up the harbour, using back roads to visit the ghosts of the past, such as the Mangungu Mission House, and Horeke, a tiny settlement with a few buildings still standing on stilts in the river (and thence to SH1).

▲ *ABOVE: A roadside sign warns motorists to look out for kiwi while driving in the kauri forests of Northland. The birds are active at night.*

▶ *OPPOSITE: Significant kauri trees, from top left: Tane Mahuta (king of the forest), Te Matua Ngahere (father of the forest), both at Waipoua; and the McKinney kauri in Parry Kauri Park, at Warkworth off SH1.*

THE LARGEST TREES

The largest kauri is Tane Mahuta, believed to be more than 1800 years old. It has a timber volume of 244.5 cubic metres, its height is 51.5 metres and the clear trunk height is 17.68 metres with a girth of 13.77 metres.

Te Matua Ngahere, the father of the forest, has a greater girth than Tane Mahuta, at 16.41 metres, but its trunk is much less at 10.21 metres, and its height is 29.9 metres.

The largest recorded kauri was almost twice the size of Tane Mahuta. Named Kairaru, it stood 30.48 metres to the first branch and was 20.12 metres round. When discovered on the slopes of Tutamoe in the late 1800s, it was believed to be the largest tree (by timber volume) in the world. It was burnt down in a bush fire.

BAYS & ISLANDS

State Highway 1 is the major route north, bypassing the huge Kaipara Harbour in the west (pages 55–59) and following up the central spine of the island. After leaving Warkworth (and its coasts; see pages 36–44) the road passes through forest patches and farmed country before entering Northland proper over the winding Brynderwyn Hills.

The view over the top looks north to Whangarei Harbour with its oil refinery and Mt Manaia (589 metres) on the north side. The peak is one of a series of eroded pinnacles, standing like the stone ancestral figures they represent, near the heads. The harbour varies from 3–6.5 kilometres wide, winding up 45 kilometres to Whangarei.

Offshore, Captain Cook's Hen and Chickens Islands are closed sanctuaries protecting populations of stitchbirds and saddlebacks along with rare petrels, shearwaters and tuatara. This pattern of offshore islands, often wildlife sanctuaries, continues up the east coast.

The Poor Knights Islands, volcanic stumps, stand 25 kilometres off Tutakaka (reached on a side road). They are both absolute sanctuaries for nature and plants, and also part of a marine reserve where divers often encounter tropical species which have drifted south on the warm currents. Cruise boats can enter one great cavern and turn around in it.

Surrounded by steep cliffs and scarred with sea caves and arches, the rocky shores fall sheer, underwater, up to 90 metres in places. Corals grow on the underwater cliffs.

The islands' rarities include the Poor Knights lily, with its curving scarlet flower stalk, found elsewhere only on neighbouring Taranga (Hen Island) off Whangarei. Rare native lizards and tuatara live among the rocks.

The group is also the only nesting place of the migrating Buller's shearwater, populations of which circumnavigate the Pacific as far as the Arctic from May each year. Also known as the New Zealand shearwater, Buller's are on the Poor Knights from mid-September and October, preparing their nests, and return to lay eggs in late November. Their population is estimated at 2.5 million birds, sharing less than 200 hectares of islets with breeding fairy prions.

The general rule of taking side roads from SH1 to reach specific harbours applies in particular to the Bay of Islands.

◀ OPPOSITE: *Piercy Island at the mouth of the Bay of Islands. Cruise boats motor through the Hole in the Rock, when conditions allow.*

▲ ABOVE: *A few homes sit on the magnificent bays on the southern shores of the Bay of Islands.*

▶ OPPOSITE, TOP: *Motuarohia or Roberton Island. A lagoon on the isthmus contains an underwater nature trail for snorkellers.*

▶ OPPOSITE, BOTTOM LEFT: *For an experience 'inside' a mangrove forest follow the boardwalk up the Waitangi River to the Haruru Falls.*

▶ OPPOSITE, BOTTOM RIGHT: *A lighthouse stands above rocky Cape Brett at the southern entrance to the Bay of Islands.*

Turn to the east coast by way of SH11 at Kawakawa (the town with a vintage railway line up the main street) and wind through typical regenerating forest. These are largely shrublands of manuka and kanuka with coastal forest, along with creeks choked with mangroves.

Captain Cook named the Bay of Islands, during his circumnavigation in 1769, for obvious reasons. The broad waterways shelter some 140 named islands and islets. The drowned valleys of three large river systems make up the bay, which has a combined coastal edge of 800 kilometres. The former hills and headlands protrude from the sea as islands, born of the general rise in seawater following the melting of the last ice age, between 10,000 and 12,000 years ago.

The Bay of Islands is regarded by some as the cradle of New Zealand's human history. The Maori heritage is notable in the landscape with many hills bearing the signs of ancient walls and ditches. Whalers and timbermen made landfall at The Beach, now Russell, but in the early 1800s a notorious haul-out for adventurers. Anglican and Roman Catholic missionaries sought the allegiance of Maori. British interests centred here and New Zealand's founding treaty was signed at Waitangi. Subsequent wars led to the founding of Auckland replacing Russell as the new capital in 1841.

The low hills and forests help retain the separateness of the Bay of Islands. Introduced rosella parakeets from Australia cackle in the shrublands along with the usual range of native and introduced birds. Kiwi may be heard at night where local citizens have introduced their own 'recovery' programmes.

Some of the islands are privately owned, or regarded as reserves, but a good few are accessible by cruises and charters. The nature reserve of Te Aroha Island is even accessible by car across a causeway in the Kerikeri Inlet; it has brown kiwi, while banded rail, spotless crake and fernbird frequent the coastal vegetation.

Major sea trips head for the Hole in the Rock, a navigable curiosity through Piercy Island at the mouth of the Bay. The 'cream trip' follows the route once taken by sailing vessels collecting the product of farms for the mainland dairy factory. There are also specialised nature tours to observe seabirds, dolphins and the occasional whale which frequent these waters.

The Bay of Islands deviation from SH1 can return to the backbone of the island, running through farmland where volcanic rock is formed into fences. Some is still stacked in piles where Maori grew sweet potato/kumara, with subtropical gourds and yams scrambling on top of the rocks

to take advantage of the reflected heat.

State Highway 1 also leads to interesting kauri forests, particularly Omahuta and Puketi which have wooden walkways giving all-weather access to big trees. Access Puketi from Waiere Road which runs from SH1 near Okaihau to SH10 near Kaeo.

Alternatively, to continue exploring the coast northward from the Bay of Islands, join SH10 at Puketona or Pakaraka and visit further drowned valleys, narrow harbours and ocean beaches. Watch for the ditches and banks of early Maori pa (forts) on the low volcanic hills. Roads off this SH10 give landward access to historic Kerikeri Inlet.

DOLPHINS OF THE BAY

The main dolphin in the Bay of Islands is the bottlenose, which is relatively common on the New Zealand coast. Bottlenose are big by dolphin standards, up to 4 metres in length. Usually travelling in groups of up to 30, the dolphins tolerate the cruise boats and, when conditions are suitable, people are able to swim with them. The smaller common dolphin, gathering sometimes in many hundreds, may also visit these waters.

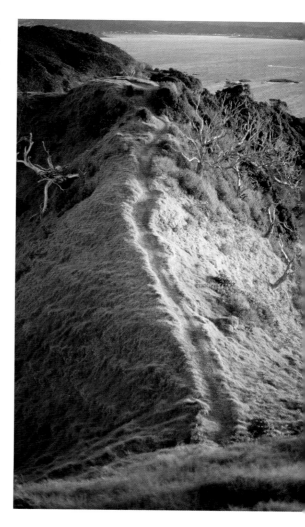

▷ *ABOVE RIGHT: Tapeka Point near Russell, Bay of Islands. The track is worn through the spreading kikuyu grass common in Northland's drier landscapes.*

▷ *RIGHT: Bottlenose dolphins follow the wake of a launch.*

◁ *OPPOSITE, TOP: Young kauri grove in Puketi Forest.*

◁ *OPPOSITE, BOTTOM: The sweeping beach of Mimiwhangata Farm Park.*

FARTHEST NORTH

The country north of Kaitaia is known as Te Aupouri Peninsula. In the alternative geography it is Te Ika a Maui, the tail of Maui's fish, curving up into the Pacific like the tail of a skate (see page 166). It is a country of giant sandhills defined in the west by Ninety Mile Beach and in the east by broad sand-bound harbours.

The land itself has been built up by the northward drift of offshore sand, linking the 'mainland' with a series of volcanic hills, once separate islands to the north. The countryside, more recently clothed in forests of manuka shrublands and peat bogs, has been slowly brought into cultivation, but it is poor land.

Consequently, extensive forests of exotic pines have been planted over much of the unstable dunelands. The wetlands and unkempt paddocks have been drained and the peatlands dried under the steady winds.

An interesting way of making this journey is by coach tour, originating as far south as the Bay of Islands. The bus has the capability of running through the huge sandhills and along the sands of Ninety Mile Beach, which are otherwise quite capable of swallowing a car.

The road up north passes through low rolling country and some small Maori settlements. These are old gumlands where pioneer diggers sought the 'fossil' gum of the great kauri trees buried in prehistoric times. Many of the gum-diggers came from the Dalmatian coast of Croatia, escaping from the old Austrian Empire, from the late 1880s. Along with the 'hard up' of many nations they probed the leached gumlands to find buried trees and kauri gum.

Working as teams they drained much of the swampland to reach deposits of the gum. Their evenings were spent in small communities of mud and sacking huts, scraping the dirt off the gum to expose the nuggets of resin. So much was collected that in the late nineteenth century kauri gum was the largest export of the whole Auckland Province, even taking account of the goldfields of the Coromandel. Gumdigger's Park features the ruins of a gumfield near Awanui.

Another contemporary industry involves digging up the remnants of kauri forests believed to have been felled by cataclysms 50,000 and 30,000 years ago. Preserved in the peat, these trees are sometimes raised with their foliage still fresh and green. The Ancient Kauri Kingdom at Awanui treats this timber, which is still strong enough to be used for fine furniture and decoration.

◀ LEFT: *Maitai Bay, a recreation reserve on the Karikari Peninsula, east off SH10.*

▲ *ABOVE: Cape Reinga from the lighthouse. The Tasman Sea, from the west, and the Pacific Ocean mix here in a turmoil of tides.*

RETURN TO HAWAIKI

The spirits of the Maori dead come here after a three-day journey northward, climbing down to Te Reinga and leaping into the ocean from an overhanging pohu-tukawa tree. From there they travel below the waves to their ancestral spirit home of Hawaiki.

From the road are distant prospects of the east coast where again sand drifts have joined offshore islets to the mainland, creating large but shallow harbours. Rangaunu and the Kaimaumau swamp are preserves for migratory birds from beyond the Arctic Circle besides a rich range of New Zealand wetland and wader species. Mount Camel is joined to the land sheltering the Houhora Harbour. The extensive white sand bars and dunes of the Parengarenga Harbour are the focus for the Maori settlement of Te Hapua. These remote harbours shelter many wading birds, including Arctic migrants.

Beyond Te Kao and Te Paki the road winds out to Cape Reinga (Te Rerenga i Wairua), the departing place of the spirits.

From the lighthouse, high on the cliffs above, observe the warring waves of the Pacific and Tasman seas turning the ocean into conflicting currents. To the left is Cape Maria van Diemen; the name is the only one that survives among those bestowed by the explorer Abel Janszoon Tasman, who sailed along the coast, without landing, in 1642. To the right is the sandy curve of Spirits Bay, some 5 kilometres long. Far beyond is the virtually inaccessible northernmost tip of New Zealand, North Cape. There, cliffs of ultramafic rock, rich in minerals, plunge nearly 200 metres into the sea. Along the clifftops and down some of the faces grows a host of shrubs and plants, specially adapted to these conditions. Several are peculiar to this place. There is no public access.

At one geological stage the higher land of the Far North comprised a group of islands. Thus unique plants evolved in isolation from the 'mainland' further south. Then the drifting sands joined them to the rest of Northland.

▼ BELOW: Blowholes in a reef on the tour-bus route along Ninety Mile Beach.

▼ BOTTOM: Looking toward Cape Maria van Diemen, named by Dutch navigator Abel Tasman in 1642. He sailed up the west coast but didn't land in New Zealand.

▲ TOP: *Rare native hibiscus plants grow in the sandhills of Te Horo Beach, Spirits Bay. The area is accessible off SH1, through Waitiki Landing.*

▲ ABOVE: *Manuka flowers in shades of pink and red, instead of white, in the far north.*

▶ OPPOSITE, TOP: *The sprawling arms of Parengarenga Harbour, formed by rising sea levels at the end of the last ice age.*

Much of the land has been burnt over, again and again. In Te Paki National Reserve the more exposed land is covered in low shrublands, including manuka and wiwi rushes.

Some gullies, passed over by the fires, have patches of re-emergent forest. These include a plot of white rata, found nowhere else. In the sandhills of Spirits Bay, the New Zealand hibiscus may be found. It is a scraggy plant about a metre high with delicate lemon flowers with black centres.

Manuka in this area blooms with a pink tinge, unlike the white of other places. Some rich-red garden varieties originated here.

The Far North has its own snail too, with a substantial turret-shaped but lopsided shell; it is called the flax snail, and lives at the root of those plants. Fossil shells of these *Placostylus* snails, faded to white, occur in Maori middens (rubbish tips) and in sandhills. The snails and their shells are absolutely protected.

The tour buses take a dramatic trip, one way or the other, depending on the tide. Driving off SH1 they plunge into the sandhills and down the course of the Te Paki stream to reach Ninety Mile Beach. Their journey follows the beach which, incidentally, is not 90 miles long but still an impressive 103 kilometres (64 miles). The only interruption is a reef protruding into the sea which features substantial blowholes.

Ninety Mile Beach ends at Ahipara near Kaitaia. Standing above it are the remains of the Ahipara Gumlands, where some 50,000 hectares of exhausted soil are reserved as a record of where the gumdiggers dug and washed kauri gum.

LAKE OHIA

Lake Ohia is a curious wetland where SH10 branches onto the Karekare Peninsula. Water levels have been manipulated over the years for farming and for conflicting conservation causes. The shallow lake overlies a devastated kauri forest, perhaps 30,000 years old. The roots of giant trees and some trunks lie exposed on the surface of the mud. A metre-high Australian orchid established here from seeds blown across the Tasman, and grew on the kauri roots when the lake was drained. Later people wanted to flood the swamp again to protect the ancient timbers.

▲ *ABOVE: Subfossil kauri logs and stumps revealed in a drained swamp, Lake Ohia.*

COROMANDEL
PENINSULA

COROMANDEL PENINSULA

The Coromandel Peninsula is rather like an island, its marching volcanic peaks falling steeply to the sea. Its western shore abuts the Firth of Thames with a long view toward Auckland. Its eastern shore, on the Bay of Plenty, has rocky headlands and long-running white sands, often containing the mouths of extensive estuaries.

Touring requires a plan because the two sides of some harbours can be many kilometres apart. There is no continuous loop road touching on all the popular beaches and dramatic landscapes. Winding roads can curve inland around the back of estuaries before returning to access the adjacent stretch of coast, often by a side road.

The Coromandel Ranges continue the line of the Kaimai–Mamaku Ranges running north from the volcanic plateau. Their origin is volcanic and the craggy slopes, deeply eroded into gorges and ridges, often peak at a remnant volcanic plug.

Mt Moehau (892 metres), at the tip of the peninsula, is fundamentally a greywacke ridge but it continues the northward line of mountains. This chain re-emerges from the sea at Cuvier Island, and at Great Barrier Island, 20 kilometres northward into the Pacific (see page 45).

The high mountain ranges of the Coromandel Peninsula are barely separated from those running up from the central North Island. The twisting Karangahake Gorge carries the road through the mountains from the Bay of Plenty to the Hauraki Plains by way of a steep-walled canyon sometimes only 100 metres across. The steep valleys and gullies either side of the bouncing Karangahake River have been mined for gold using hard-rock methods, and the remains of the workings can still be visited on short trails.

▶ OPPOSITE, TOP: *The twisting, narrow road up the western Coromandel coast is lined with pohutukawa trees that hang over the road and the sea.*

▶ OPPOSITE, BOTTOM: *Flax bushes provide a margin to the sea at Hot Water Beach, eastern Coromandel. Scrape a hole near the low tide and enjoy the thermal hot water.*

◀ PAGES 74–75: *Cathedral Cove scenic reserve is a popular picnic and swimming spot off the main road near Hahei, south of Whitianga. Volcanic ignimbrite forms the fragile framework of the cliffs, caves and islets.*

▲ *ABOVE: Working model of a kauri dam in the Kauaeranga Valley south of Thames. Such dams across mountain valleys built up a head of water to propel felled timber downstream.*

The Paeroa end of the gorge sits alongside the edge of an ancient graben, or sunken land block, which has down-faulted to form the Hauraki Plains and the ensuing Firth of Thames along the peninsula's west coast. Captain Cook entered the river in 1769 in the course of his search for trees to make masts and spars but could find no kauri. Instead the riverbanks were lined with even taller trees, kahikatea, which is too soft for structural purposes. It was the 1920s before the plains were fully cleared for farming and the swamps drained. The high tide still backs up the rivers and creeks for more than 30 kilometres so gentle is the slope of the Thames Valley.

Thames, the commercial centre of the region, stands at the mouth of the Kauaeranga River, a centre of the old timber industry. The river valley remains the pathway back into the mountain gorges. There, visitors can enjoy the preserved forests and the atmosphere of the kauri-milling days, on display at the information centre some 13 kilometres in.

In this area kauri millers constructed wooden dams on the narrow side streams and built up a huge head of water to help 'drive' the timber downstream to the mills. When the dams were 'tripped' a wall of water rushed down the gorges, moving the trunks to the recovery point. Ruins of the kauri dams, and other historic features of the kauri timber days, are highlights of the walking tracks.

Thames town itself grew on the substance of kauri milling and gold mining. It occupies a flat at the foot of the mountains where crushing plants boomed from the 1880s to the early 1900s. Much of the town is built on land reclaimed from the sea with mining waste. Seashore birds still roost here at high tide.

The road from Thames to Coromandel town begins along the sea side just above the rocky shore. It is a narrow and winding way, often round headlands where remnant groves of coastal pohutukawa trees shade the road. Fast local traffic and unexpected timber trucks and trailers call for defensive driving.

The hills here often rise sheer from the shore, except where a narrow stream interrupts, crossed by a one-way bridge. The early beach settlements of old cottages cling to the hillsides overlooking the Firth.

Generally the hills are overgrown with exotic plants, with occasional patches of exotic pines and macrocarpa. Near Tararu, hundreds of shags nest in trees high above the road. Watch for flocks of shearwaters and petrels out in the Firth, accompanied perhaps by diving white-fronted terns and golden-capped gannets which nest on islands further along the coast. Shingle bars at river mouths can contain semi-precious stones such as carnelians, agate, jasper and chalcedony.

At length the road rises onto hillsides overhung by rocky volcanic bluffs and overlooking the invading arms of the sea. The islands scattered offshore are the remnants of hills drowned by rising sea levels at the end of the ice ages.

The estuaries and shores of places like Manaia and Coromandel Harbour are the haunt of many wading and wetland birds. Some of the ubiquitous godwits and knots feed here on mudflats, along with various species of duck. The booming Australasian bittern hides in the crush of bulrush or raupo. The pukeko, known as the purple gallinule elsewhere, is conspicuous. Fernbirds, rails and crakes move through the rushes and small mangroves. Banded rail may cross the roads, looking like elongated chickens as they run.

From the vicinity of Coromandel town there are several routes, either north further up the west coast, or across the peninsula to access places on the east coast. The road north to Colville is classed as a secondary highway. From there it is a corrugated dirt road, practically one way, and difficult driving, round the base of Mt Moehau.

COOK NAMES

Lieutenant James Cook named a number of islands in the Bay of Plenty as he sailed the *Endeavour* up the east coast of the Coromandel in 1769.

One group, where pillars of rock stand above the sea like an assembly of councillors, was named the Court of Aldermen. Cook dubbed nearby Tuhua (see 'Tuhua — isle of glass' page 82) Mayor Island.

He also named some islets after Mercury, the planet observed by his expedition. This name was later transferred to the present Mercury group, replacing Les Iles de Haussez, a name given by the French explorer Dumont d'Urville about 1827.

Great Mercury is the fifth-biggest island off the mainland coast after Great Barrier (see page 44) and is privately owned. Its smaller companions in the group, the six other Mercuries, are difficult to access and are nature reserves for seabirds, insects, lizards and tuatara.

The Great and Little Barrier islands, which help protect the waters of the Hauraki Gulf, north of the Coromandel, were also named by Cook.

The forests above are often clouded in mist. Their mysterious atmosphere has encouraged tales such as the local legend of 'Moehau man', a hairy ginger giant who haunts the cloud forests. Tama te Kapua, commander of the migratory Maori canoe Aotea, is buried high on its subalpine crest where bogs and stunted growth reflect the plant life of more southerly mountains.

Along the highlands of the Coromandel

▲ *ABOVE:* *Understorey plants flourish in the light penetrating the rainforest along this streamside on Mt Moehau.*

Peninsula, plants peculiar to the cooler climates of the southern North Island blend with those of the subtropical north. As a consequence, more than 350 species of plants and trees have been recorded on the peninsula.

The wildlife is often rich. Restoration projects involving pest control sustain extensive kiwi sanctuaries. The experimental release of some 20 brown teal at Port Jackson produced a population of more than 200 of this endangered duck within just five years.

The wet forests of Moehau hold two species of New Zealand's four endangered native frogs: Archey's frog and Hochstetter's frog. New Zealand's native frogs appear to break the rules

for this amphibian group, in not having a free-swimming tadpole stage. Instead froglets hatch directly from eggs carried by the male.

Archey's frog frequents damp corners under cover on the forest floor. Like the other local species of frogs it is susceptible to a chytrid fungal disease which has further threatened the remaining populations. With only two known populations, Archey's frog is critically endangered, and believed to be on the brink of extinction.

The roads across the Coromandel Ranges are steep and winding. They are also discontinuous so choose your route with care. An unsealed minor road just north of Colville clambers over the shoulder of Mt Moehau to reach Port Charles and Stony Bay on the east coast; it also branches south to Waikawa Bay and Kennedy Bay before returning over the mountains again to Coromandel town. Long stretches of the east coast have no roads, though there are distant glimpses of beach, reef and fringing islands from the hillsides.

Highway 25 from Coromandel crosses the ranges and gives access to a suite of extensive beaches, harbours and estuaries where birds gather. The white sands and dunes are the breeding grounds of native waders such as the New Zealand red-breasted dotterel and the variable (black) oystercatcher. Foreign bird migrants also visit the tidal flats in summer. Fernbirds, spotless crakes and banded rails may be found on the marshlands, along with occasional bitterns and duck.

Much of the forest on the Coromandel is only regenerating after the depredations of millers and miners from the 1880s to the 1920s. Cone-shaped native rewarewa rise as emergent forest above shrub species including coprosmas, pittosporum, manuka, kanuka and tree ferns. Puriri, totara, kahikatea and infant kauri struggle to re-establish here. Too often, introduced gorse and wilding pine have taken over the cleared spaces.

Whenuakite Conservation Reserve is a milled-over native forest in recovery. Local conservationists have promoted a kiwi sanctuary here, trapping pests and encouraging forest regeneration over 3000 hectares.

The explorer James Cook visited and named Mercury Bay in 1769. Cook chose to go ashore on what is now Cooks Beach, south of Whitianga, to take astronomical readings of the transit of the planet Mercury across the sun. This allowed the calculation of a known latitude for New Zealand.

The town of Whitianga in Mercury Bay

▲ TOP: *The Coromandel road follows the seashore out of Thames.*

▲ ABOVE: *A short passenger-ferry trip across the Whitianga River saves nearly an hour of driving around the head of the river to reach the houses on the other side.*

TUHUA — ISLE OF GLASS

Tuhua, the Maori name for volcanic glass or obsidian, lies a 27-kilometre helicopter flight off the eastern Coromandel, in the Bay of Plenty. The 1277-hectare island is the steep-sided stump of an ancient volcano with two crater lakes at its centre.

Black glass flakes chipped from reefs of obsidian on the island are found in Maori waste tips in many parts of New Zealand. Obsidian flakes were used as tools for scraping, cutting and eating, and the glass chips were traded throughout New Zealand in pre-European times.

▲ TOP: The twin cones of Paku at Tairua, eastern Coromandel Peninsula, have been ringed with houses. They look down on the beach settlement and across a narrow entrance to the 'suburbs' of Pauanui. Signs near the top of Paku warn of a resident kiwi population in the nearby scrub.

▲ ABOVE: Flocks of white-fronted terns frequent the Coromandel shores. Fishers know them as kahawai birds for they follow shoals of these fish.

is only 100-odd metres by passenger ferry from the southern shore at Shakespear Head. The road journey up river and back again, to reach the settlements on the other side, can take an hour or more by car.

Along this coast bands of volcanic ignimbrite form white cliffs in places, particularly at much-visited Cathedral Cove near Hahei.

Hot springs under the surf at Hot Water Beach can be enjoyed by digging a hole in the sand two hours either side of low tide.

The double peak of Paku stands at the mouth of the Tairua Harbour, overlooking the holiday settlement of Tairua. The marine suburbia of Pauanui lies across the river, again a short ferry ride though several kilometres away by road round the harbour.

Nearby, the Kopu–Hikuai road crosses the mountainous peninsula again. The bendy but modern road climbs through regrowth forest, linking the Bay of Plenty with Thames and the road to Auckland.

Highway 25 runs further south, however, with access to several more coastal resorts and good birding in the estuaries. The road then turns inland and runs from Waihi to Paeroa on the Hauraki Plains, passing through the Waikino and Karangahake gorges, with their remnants of the old gold workings.

▶ RIGHT, TOP: *A sideroad off SH25 at Kuaotunu leads to a series of eastern bays and beaches, including Opito Bay.*

▶ RIGHT, CENTRE: *The extensive Coromandel Harbour is protected by several offshore islands.*

▶ RIGHT: *The Karangahake Gorge, between Waihi and Paeroa, separates the Coromandel Peninsula from the inland Kaimai Ranges.*

BAY OF PLENTY

ROTORUA

The thermal region round Rotorua is also the centre of a lakeland wilderness.

Volcanic activity has shaped the Rotorua region; its mudpools, hot springs and geysers are continuing reminders that this place sits over an unstable part of the earth's crust. The major eruption of Mt Tarawera in 1886 scattered ash across the land, stripping forests of their foliage, and killing an estimated 105 people. Yet beneath the brooding mountain lies a chain of apparently tranquil lakes, habitat for a rich range of birds.

Earlier eruptions in the region produced layers of ash that blanketed the land. On other occasions fiery clouds of gas and ash exploded across the landscape, running overland like an avalanche, cooling to set in reefs of ignimbrite rock.

The great Mamaku plateau which rises from the south Waikato farmlands on the way to Rotorua was laid down by such a 'pyroclastic' flow. Much of the soil in the region is only a thin layer of humus formed in the past few hundred years. The walls of road cuttings show that close beneath the surface lie successive layers of volcanic material, laid down over the millennia, including sometimes the charred remnants of burnt and buried forests of the past.

▼ *BELOW: At Waiotapu, steam drifts off a colourful series of hot springs and pools, including the Champagne Pool with its effervescent bubbles.*

Reminders of this violent and recent past can be seen throughout the Rotorua Lakes district in the frequent outbreaks of thermal activity.

Approaching Rotorua by SH5, the hilltop farmland is marked by curious standing stones. These are actually the eroded plugs of small volcanoes. The highway then runs down into the Rotorua caldera, to the lake and the city.

In Rotorua city the pervasive smell of rotten eggs can be traced directly to the hydrogen sulphide escaping from inside the earth by way of hot springs, mudpools and other volcanic phenomena. Thermal steam escapes from underground not only at the well-known field at Whakarewarewa but in suburban streets, by the lakeside, and in corners of the golf course. The generous parks and reserves which surround the central city have often been set aside because the land is simply too fragile or unsafe to build on.

The huge boiling aquifer under the city was for many years tapped by householders and businesses as a source of cheap heat, but the decay of geysers and hot springs at Whakarewarewa led to the closure of many private bores during the 1980s. Since then, thermal activity has revived.

Rotorua city is built on the floor of a huge volcanic caldera which contains the waters of its namesake lake. Originally the area was the roof of a vast underground basin of volcanic magma which erupted some 220,000 years ago. The caldera was created when the roof of the emptied bowl fell in, after the release of the ignimbrite which formed the Mamaku plateau. Varied lake levels over the intervening millennia may be traced

▲ TOP: *The rim of the Champagne Pool is coloured by a deposit of antimony and arsenic.*

▲ ABOVE: *One of the largest hot springs in the world, Frying Pan Lake occupies the Echo Crater at Waimangu. Numerous hot springs under the lake heat its 3.8 hectares.*

◀ PAGES 84–85: *Volcanic and thermal wonders draw visitors to the Rotorua district. Three species of gull roost and nest on the thermal foreshore of Sulphur Bay.*

▲ *ABOVE: This steaming stream at Waimangu is too hot to touch.*

in terraces surrounding the basin, which is some 15 kilometres across.

A more ancient caldera, known as the Okataina caldera, lies to the east of Rotorua. Its original basin shape has been modified by subsequent volcanic activity on its floor including the formation of the domes of the Haroharo and Tarawera volcanoes.

The Rotorua suburb of Ohinemutu, a celebrated Maori settlement on the lake shore, sits in an active field of hot springs. Just around the corner of Hospital Hill, Kuirau Park contains steaming lakes, mudpools and hot springs. On the golf course near Whakarewarewa, mudpools and mud volcanoes form unusual hazards.

The Government Gardens, on the eastern side of the town, contain more steaming phenomena spreading along the shore of the lake. The Priest Spring has been harnessed to heat the Polynesian Pools.

Whakarewarewa lies at the edge of the ancient Rotorua caldera and is the source of much of the hot water welling up under pressure from an underground fault. Deep down it may be over 240°C, creating the superheated steam that fires the geysers.

Whakarewarewa reserve contains some 500 hot springs within its square-kilometre bounds. Te Puia Flat with its geysers is the most famous feature but there is a fascinating array of hot pools and boiling mud scattered through the peculiar shrubland that survives in the heated earth. Orchids and other small plants flourish on the rim of pits filled with bubbling mud.

Maori houses next door sit on soil which may be heated from 70–90°C by the geothermal energy below. Maori residents still use the blue chloride pools for cooking and bathing, according to the water temperature. Of necessity, their ancestors are buried in overground tombs.

Te Puia Flat has seven active geysers along a terrace of white sinter but not all of them erupt regularly. Mahanga, the Boxing Glove, is the most frequent, punching up several metres. The angled Prince of Wales Feathers blows almost continuously. Overall, the great Pohutu Geyser erupts to a height of 18–20 metres or more.

Sinter, a rock formed from silica precipitated from the thermal water, covers the surface of Te Pura Flat and spills like a white stone waterfall to the warm river below.

The drained bores of other geysers nearby are a reminder of the unstable nature of the area. Some contain blue chloride water.

Among the swirling mudpools, the Frog Pool or Ngamokaiakoko is best known. Mud leaps off the surface in gobs looking like leaping frogs. In dry seasons the surface mud hardens, building up mud volcanoes which continually erupt mud from below.

East of Rotorua, Hell's Gate or Tikitere is promoted as the most active thermal field. It occupies a 20-hectare site rising from the Whakatane road (SH30) and includes several extremely hot mudpools and lakes. The Inferno reaches 105°C. The Steaming Cliffs have temperatures of 122°C. A hot waterfall drains an extensive lake, tumbling through ferns and shrubs. The yellow deposits of sulphur contrast with the black, boiling mud of graphite

▲ *ABOVE: Steaming earth and boiling mud are features of Hell's Gate, Tikitere.*

pools. Muds mined here are sold for cosmetic purposes.

The thermal fields south of Rotorua are equally spectacular. Waimangu is reached on a loop road from the Rotorua–Taupo SH5. This is the valley of craters formed when Tarawera erupted in 1886.

South Crater is full now with cold water, but adjacent to it the Echo Crater contains Frying Pan Lake, one of the largest hot-water springs in the world. This was once known as Frying Pan Flat, until the area erupted again in 1917, destroying the tourist centre and scalding two of the occupants to death.

The surface of the lake is swept by steam and bubbles as heated water rises from vents some 6 metres underwater. A spectacular steaming cliff face is aptly described as the Cathedral Rocks.

Close by, the Inferno Crater is almost enclosed by sheer cliffs surrounding the bright blue waters of Ruaumoko's Throat

▲ *ABOVE: Tarawera in eruption, early in the morning of June 10, 1886. This chromolithograph was engraved from a painting by Charles Blomfield. It shows the eruption of several vents along the domes of Tarawera. Mud and steam on the right mark the eruption of drowned lake craters towards Waimangu.*

(Ruaumoko being the god of volcanoes). The water here rises and falls 8 or 9 metres in a 38-day cycle, spilling into a hot-water stream. It was close to here that the world's largest geyser erupted between 1900 and 1904. The Waimangu (black water) Geyser shot muddy water and rocks more than 450 metres into the sky.

The walking track (or the internal bus service) runs down to the shores of Lake Rotomahana, itself eight times larger than it was before the Tarawera eruption. A launch cruise on the lake passes over the sites of the once world-famous Pink and

TARAWERA ERUPTS

The Tarawera eruption of 1886 was just one of a series of eruptions that began with the origin of the volcano only 18,000 years ago. Subsequent eruptions some 15,000, 11,000 and 600–700 years ago built the several domes of Mt Tarawera as a complex of volcanoes. The eruption of 1886 was different, being explosive, producing red and black basalt which overlays the earlier white rhyolite on the crater walls. An 8 kilometres rift across the crest of the domes extended into lakes Okaro and Rotomahana. New volcanic craters opened up all the way to Waimangu, creating a volcanic rift 15.9 kilometres long. The noise of the eruption was heard as far away as Auckland and Christchurch.

Volcanic fall-out from the volcano reached coastal Bay of Plenty and Napier. Close to the mountain, ash deposits reached 45 metres deep, burying some Maori settlements by Lake Tarawera. At Te Wairoa, buildings collapsed under the pressure of a metre and more of mud from the water-filled craters, creating what can be visited today as the Buried Village.

▲ TOP LEFT: *Rare Maori stone store, excavated at the Buried Village.*

▲ TOP: *The reds and whites of the Tarawera chasm illustrate phases of its volcanic history. The darker basalt material was generated by the 1886 eruption; the white rhyolite dates from the earlier eruptions which formed the domes. The volcano now has a series of craters over its 18 kilometre length, beginning here under the dome of Wahanga and extending for 8 kilometres along the crest of the mountain, and down its western flank into water-filled Rotomahana and the craters of the Waimangu Valley.*

▲ ABOVE: *Excavated Maori house at the Buried Village.*

ROTORUA REDWOODS

On the southern fringe of Rotorua, an arboretum originally developed for forest research demonstrates the encouraging conditions that many introduced species of tree find in New Zealand. The arboretum was begun in 1899 with the planting of 170 different species from around the world. The Californian redwoods were planted in 1901 and now reach over 60 metres in height. The 6 hectares of redwoods are now part of a city-owned forest park at Whakarewarewa which offers extensive walks and bike trails.

▲ *ABOVE: Redwoods at Whakarewarewa, on the outskirts of Rotorua.*

White Terraces which were shattered and scattered by the blasts.

Further south, the Waiotapu thermal reserve is also located on a loop road from SH5. It is part of a thermal field which begins at the Rainbow Mountain (Maungakakaramea) and extends over some 18 square kilometres southward into the Reporoa district (another caldera). Walking through its wild landscape leads to a view out over water-filled explosion craters towards the steam plumes of the Reporoa geothermal stations.

Waiotapu contains spectacular craters from past geysers and underground collapses. Its rich and varied colours, which often stain the ponds, reflect the minerals brought to the surface by geothermal activity. Fumaroles expelling gas from underground are often ringed by deposits of yellow sulphur. Antimony and arsenic produce a bright orange rim just inside the Champagne Pool. The run-off from the pool flows across a white sinter terrace stained yellow in places. Red earth contains iron oxides. Oily surfaced black inkwells may be coloured by iron sulphides, or by natural oil and carbon from ancient vegetable matter buried below. Green may be the product of ferrous iron or sulphur in solution.

At the Champagne Pool, carbon dioxide bubbles to the surface of a small lake standing on a platform of silica. As the water overflows it deposits silica over extensive flats, mixing in places with springs which produce the various coloured pools of the Artist's Palette. The sinter slopes off into the Lavender Terraces, delicately growing formations each with a tiny lip over which the thermal water gradually descends onto a tumbling waterfall. Beyond lies a series of explosion craters, containing colourful springs and fumaroles, with Lake Ngakoro and Green Lake beyond.

Also on the Waiotapu Loop Road is a spectacular mudpool, with active explosions of mud leaping a metre and more like giant boiling porridge. Nearby, the Lady Knox Geyser is guaranteed to perform. At 10.15 every morning the former hot pool is induced to erupt by its caretakers adding soap to an artificially narrowed vent.

The scatter of lakes through the Rotorua district is the by-product of the volcanic nature of the land. Lake levels have fluctuated with the changing earth,

eruptions damming some and creating others.

Rotorua Lake, some 12 by 10 kilometres, is the most prominent. Rotorua flows into smaller Rotoiti, which in turn drains over the Okere Falls into the Kaituna River and the Bay of Plenty. Rotoiti has shoreline hot springs, reminders of the volcanic origin. Beyond Rotoiti on SH30 are two smaller lakes, Rotoehu and Rotoma.

Lake Okataina can be reached by a picturesque forest road from Rotoehu. Its 3 kilometre road tunnel of tree fuchsia full of bellbirds has changed in nature in recent years following the onslaught of possums, and the fuchsia has been replaced with hardier species. The lake itself has changed in level since

EXOTIC PINE FORESTS

Much of the forest surrounding Rotorua is of introduced pine trees, particularly *Pinus radiata* or Monterey pine originally from coastal California. These trees mature to harvest size in 25–28 years and are the basis of the exotic timber industry.

Radiata pine was first introduced to New Zealand around 1860, originally for quick shelter. Its rapid growth and tolerance of harsh conditions saw it planted widely, in places as varied as moving sandhills to chilly mountainsides.

Some commercial plots were planted in the early 1900s. Vast plantations were established during the work schemes of the 1930s and in another boom in the 1960s.

Radiata pine provides the raw material for a $2.5 billion dollar export industry. Its uses extend from pulp and paper products to building construction and furniture, joinery,

panels and cladding.

The Whakarewarewa Forest on the southern edge of Rotorua extends from The Redwoods to surround the Blue and Green lakes in 5667 hectares of mainly radiata forest which offers walking and riding tracks.

To the southeast of Rotorua the pine forests extend onto the Kaingaroa Plains, where there are 110,000 hectares of plantation forest, nearly three-quarters of it in radiata pine.

The lower branches of production trees are trimmed to create tall poles and the plantation is thinned at 14 years. Mature trees are clearfelled and replanted.

Tree ferns and native shrubs often grow below the canopy of pines as an understorey. The exotic forests provide habitat for small bush birds, and introduced species such as possums, pigs and red deer.

NATIVE FORESTS

The forests which surround Rotorua and its lakes include extensive plantings of introduced pines and larches, the basis of today's timber industry. Native forests were cleared for plantations until the 1980s. Extensive native forest survives on the Kaimai–Mamaku Range, however, on the SH5 route from the Waikato to Rotorua.

At first there are fine prospects of tawa and other hardwood forest. Much of the Mamaku forest has been logged and here, as elsewhere in the Lakes district, the dense but low forest is the product of natural reafforestation. It is rich in shrub species, ferns and vines.

Maori burnt much of the tall forest around the lakes to establish gardens and beds of bracken fern, the roots of which were a staple food. Loggers took most of the remaining large rimu and kahikatea.

The columnar rewarewa, with its purple bottlebrushes in spring, is a common tree in this region for it is one of the pioneer species which spring first in new forests. Look for the occasional reserves of tall trees to capture something of the natural forest type of yesteryear.

the Tarawera eruption when it rose 12 metres. During the 1960s, divers located the palisades of a sunken Maori village beneath its waters. Access around its forested shores is by walking track or launch.

The road from Rotorua to Lake Tarawera (Tarawera Road at Lynmore) passes Lake Tikitapu (Blue Lake) and Rotokakahi (Green Lake). Pause on the isthmus between them, once a Maori fortress, and compare the colours. A loop road also reaches into Lake Okareka, with its settled verge and rich birdlife.

Lake Tarawera lies below the often cloud-capped mass of the Tarawera volcanoes. Its surface is said to have risen prior to the eruption of 1886, and tourists on the lake caught a glimpse of a phantom canoe rowing toward the tribal burial ground below the mountain.

Away to the south of Tarawera, overlooking the Kaingaroa Plains, lies Lake Rerewhakaaitu which has no natural outlet. Access is by a side road off SH5 which leaves at the colourful earth of Rainbow Mountain. Its surrounding wetlands provide interesting waterbird habitat.

Indeed, all the lakes provide good bird habitat. In Rotorua itself, a wildlife refuge protects the breeding ground of three kinds of gull. These are largely red-billed gulls but the increasingly rare South Island species, the black-billed gull, also nests on the steaming volcanic flats near the Polynesian Pools. A lakeside walkway round the Government Gardens gives access to the nesting and resting sites of several duck species and shags. Little black and little shags breed on dead trees on islets just offshore. Black shags, pied

stilt and the golden-eyed black teal or scaup can be seen, particularly at the road end at Motutara Point. The shoreline walk continues through manuka thickets to downtown Rotorua where black swans and various ducks proliferate.

Parking areas by several lakes are good places to look out for a range of water birds, including pukeko and Australian coot. Dabchick are fascinating to watch as they dive for food, carrying their young. Bittern occur by some lakesides, usually hidden in the raupo swamps. In wet areas of reeds and scrub, fernbirds hide, and may occasionally be seen clambering to the top of the foliage.

The usual forest birds, including tui and bellbird, can be seen along quiet tracks. Whiteheads and pied tits also occur here, and in a few forest reserves, the North Island robin. Open country and weedy patches attract European finches, including chaffinches and redpolls which may also be heard feeding in the tops of the plantations.

▲ *TOP: Te Puia (or Geyser) Flat at Whakarewarewa thermal area has seven geysers. Mahanga (the Boxing Glove) is most frequent, along with the Prince of Wales Feathers. The highest is the variable Pohutu Geyser.*

▲ *ABOVE: Native forest is recovering in the valley of the Te Wairoa stream, buried in mud by the eruption of Tarawera in 1886.*

TE UREWERA

Te Urewera National Park and its adjacent forests are as far from civilisation as it's possible to get by road. State Highway 38 runs through the wild ranges as a continuously winding, narrow road including 95 kilometres on gravel or dirt. It also crosses two major mountain ranges before it skirts Lake Waikaremoana, the accepted heart of the park. Even then only a tiny fraction of its 212,673 hectares is readily accessible.

This is lonely country where a few Maori settlements linger on valley flats on the way in, surrounded by dense native forests. Even the little areas of burnt or once-cleared land are reverting to trees again, with the soaring heads of surviving podocarp pines piercing the canopy of smaller hardwood trees.

Te Urewera National Park begins in a jumble of rugged mountains and steep forested faces. This is the beginning of the journey promoted as the Rainforest Highway, and in fairness 'rainforest' is a fair descriptor; 'highway', however, is a gross exaggeration.

The most striking features to begin with are the giant frames of rata and podocarps such as totara, matai, rimu and kahikatea standing dramatically above the general canopy of broadleaf forest. The road winds and climbs across the Ikawhenua Range only to face an even higher barrier, the Huiarau Range.

Climbing to the top, the podocarp giants give way to substantial beech trees draped in moss and lichens.

In summer the screech of long-tailed cuckoos, migrants from the Solomon Islands and Bismarck Archipelago, can be heard in the forest vastness. Their voices are ventriloquistic and it is easiest to find them by overlooking a forested valley and watching for their swooping flight above the canopy. The long-tailed cuckoo comes here to lay its eggs in the nests of the whitehead, a much smaller, sparrow-sized bird.

The shining cuckoo is another migrant from the same region, with a more intimate rising then falling call, an early sign of impending summer. The shining cuckoo is not much bigger than a sparrow and parasitises the nest of the tiny grey warbler, a hanging bag-shaped nest with an entry hole in the side.

These high forests are also the haunt of native parakeets and the kaka bush-parrot. The argumentative cackling of the kakariki, red-crowned or yellow-crowned parakeets, warns of their

◄ *OPPOSITE: Lake Waikaremoana is the major feature of Te Urewera. Its many arms reflects its origin as a series of drowned valleys.*

▲ *ABOVE: Lake Waikareiti is a gentle 300-metre climb from Aniwaniwa. Giant podo-carp pines and beech soaring over hardwood and ferns give an introduction to mature rainforest.*

CHILDREN OF THE MIST

This romantic name was perpetuated to recall the isolated Tuhoe people, who occupied the greater part of the region in pre-European times, and still do. The massive hills are frequently damp with drifting mists and recall the mating of sky and earth in primeval times, and the consequent birth of Tuhoe as a people.

approach through the high canopy. The kaka screeches, and gives itself away as it swoops heavily through the forest. These big brown birds with reddish underwings are sometimes alarmed along the track, where they feed by tearing down fruits or foliage and by ripping into rotten wood to take insects and grubs.

Observing the bush birds is best done by sitting still in the forest, preferably overlooking a gully where they come to feed. Small bush birds widespread in these forests include pied tit/toutouwai, whitehead, grey warbler, silvereye, bush robin, fantail and rifleman. The soft 'zeet' call of the tiny green rifleman draws attention as it attacks the insects on a tree trunk by zig-zagging up the bark.

Lake Waikaremoana is a broad stretch of water overlooked by the gigantic Panekiri Bluff. These are the broken outer edges of a huge mountain uplift which rises 535 metres sheer above lake level. The broken layers of rock expose faces of ancient deposits, giving the cliffs a distinctive banded appearance.

The lake itself is a former river valley, flooded some 2200 years ago when a landslide blocked its natural outflow at Onepoto on the southwest corner. The waters of the lake then back-filled the streams, flooding up the old river valleys.

Patches of lower forest show where fires have occurred over the centuries. Some of the land in the park is privately owned, including Maori sacred sites and former settlements. Access through these areas is permitted as a courtesy.

Driving along the lake, the road runs through heavy bush, high along the edge of the Ngamoko Range. Occasionally a side road descends steeply to the lakeshore, perhaps a tiny beach overhung with forest. Waterfalls plunge through the forest, notably the 37-metre Mokau Falls which are crossed by the road.

The human focus of the park is the headquarters at Aniwaniwa (and the nearby Waikaremoana motor camp complex). Excellent and varied short walks lead from here, including a descent of the Aniwaniwa Falls, and an hour uphill to little Waikare, Waikareiti. This is a smaller lake also formed by a landslide and now containing two islands, one with its own central lake.

Waikaremoana has a good population of waterbirds, various ducks and teal, black swan and white-faced heron. While possums and stoats have devastated much of the forest birdlife, there is the possibility of hearing brown kiwi screeching at night from a specially pest-controlled area near Aniwaniwa.

The motor camp (and cabins) provides a base for exploring the park. There is

CARVING THE LAKE

Maori tradition has it that Lake Waikare-moana was carved by a taniwha or water spirit. Mahu, a local chief, sent his children down to the lakeshore for water. When they took water from a sacred spring instead, their angry father turned them to stone. Mahu then took his remaining daughter Haumapuhia to the lake and tried to drown her. Unable to breathe Haumapuhia turned herself into a taniwha. In her efforts to escape she burrowed into the surrounding hills, creating the many arms of the lake. Then at Onepoto she sank underwater where she can be seen as a huge rock at the outlet of a greatly enlarged lake.

▼ BELOW: The gigantic Panekiri Bluff is the broken outer edge of a huge mountain fault. The exposed faces of ancient deposits give the cliffs a distinctive layered appearance.

an area of caves and fractured cliffs on the hillside to the south: earthquakes have fathered great rockfalls and fissures known as the Onepoto Caves above the lake.

At Onepoto the lake flows into the intake of the Tuai electric power scheme. Built a couple of kilometres downstream, toward Wairoa, the scheme initially lowered the lake level by 5 metres and now allows it to rise and fall naturally over 3 metres with the seasons.

Lake Waikaremoana Great Walk is a four- or five-day clamber around the unroaded far side of the lake. It begins at Onepoto by climbing the long slope behind Panekiri Bluff to 1150 metres with a tramping hut at the top. The walk continues through beech forest and mixed rainforest, following above the lakeshores to Hopuaruahine Landing in the north. A fast boat service takes trampers in and out if they are doing only a section of the walk; taking a lift on such a service trip opens the panorama of the lake.

A trip into Te Urewera requires some planning and reserving of accommodation. Two nights allows for access in and out and at least a full day for short walks.

There are simple general stores at Ruatahuna on the edge of the deepest forest, and on the lakeshore near Aniwaniwa. Fill fuel tanks before venturing into the region and book accommodation ahead as Aniwaniwa is heavily patronised and there are no alternatives. Dose up against car sickness and move cautiously as a slide on the shingle could dump the car into a deep watertable on inside corners or even over the edge of the sheer cliffs.

Te Urewera is not to everyone's taste, being often gloomy and subject to the extremes of temperature and weather, which change in minutes in mountain country. For those who can handle the primitive roads, and suffer the inconvenience, this is a fair taste of the wild New Zealand of pioneer times.

VISITING THE FOREST

To get to Te Urewera National Park from Rotorua take SH38, which turns off SH5 at Rainbow Mountain. The long, straight highway cuts across the Kaingaroa Forest, said to be the largest man-made forest in the world.

The pine forests were planted during the economic depression of the 1930s, covering scrubby grass plains across the outflows of the Taupo eruptions. Mainly *Pinus radiata*, native to California, the trees cover 150,000 hectares and are now completing their second generation of 35 years.

The forest journey into Te Urewera begins as the road enters the mountains east of the Kaingaroa Plains (also accessible from Whakatane). On the south side stretches the dense and rarely penetrated Whirinaki Forest, a roadless forest park backing onto Te Urewera. The Whirinaki forest sanctuary, south of Minginui, is visited by those curious to see an impressive stand of ancient podocarp trees, but the area is remote and generally not recommended.

▲ TOP LEFT: *The Onepoto Caves were formed as overhanging rocks twisted and slipped along the unstable lakeshores.*

▶ TOP RIGHT: *The Aniwaniwa Falls descend through three drops to the lake.*

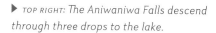
▲ ABOVE: *Mature podocarps pierce the canopy of the forest.*

▶ RIGHT: *Several short walks begin at Aniwaniwa park headquarters.*

COASTAL

BAY OF PLENTY

Named by Lieutenant James Cook, while aboard the *Endeavour* in 1769, the Bay of Plenty reflects his success in obtaining food from local Maori — after his disappointment in Poverty Bay. Today, the productive orchards and fields of the Bay of Plenty have driven the wilderness back to the adjoining ranges of Coromandel, Rotorua and Te Urewera.

The gentle curve of sandy coastline is extensively settled with coalescing beach suburbs. In places the coastal road runs along the bottom of ancient sea terraces, overhung by pohutukawa and frequented by tui and bellbird in summer.

Only a few coastal estuaries and wetlands offer the chance of 'birding'. At the Kaituna river mouth there are wetland birds and waders; the Matata lagoons and the Tarawera river mouth are other spots to find wetland birds.

The wilderness interest of the Bay of Plenty is largely contained on offshore islands which reflect their volcanic origins; there are tours by air and sea to access the most striking.

The Bay of Plenty lies at the northern edge of the Taupo Volcanic Zone. Mt Edgecumbe or Putauaki, near Kawerau, is a conspicuous cone rising to 849 metres above the inland plains. Its last eruptions date from 2000 to 5000 years ago. The line of Taupo volcanoes, however, ends under the sea far out in the bay.

Moutohora or Whale Island, 9 kilometres northwest of Whakatane, is a remnant volcanic cone and is now a wildlife management reserve. There are hot springs and fumaroles in Sulphur Bay. The 143-hectare island has been replanted in many places with native trees, since goats, rats, cats and rabbits were eradicated in the 1980s. Grey-faced

EDGECUMBE EARTHQUAKE

The Rangitaiki Plains between Matata and Whakatane were built up from volcanic material spread by local rivers. When a shallow earthquake of 6.3 magnitude struck near Edgecumbe in 1987 the surface of the earth split apart along the fault. The force opened a crack up to 1 metre wide over a length of 7 kilometres. Railway lines and roads distorted laterally. The earth on the western side of the fault dropped up to a couple of metres in some places.

▲ TOP AND ABOVE: *Inside the crater of White Island/Whakaari, an active volcano.*

▲ ABOVE: *Sulphur builds up around the fumaroles and was once mined.*

▲ TOP: *White Island viewed from the sea. The only green patch is where Australasian gannets breed in season.*

▲ ABOVE: *Steam rises continuously from the crater of New Zealand's most active volcano.*

petrels (oi or northern muttonbird) have their burrows there. Sooty shearwaters also nest. Threatened and rare species include the North Island saddleback or tieke which has been relocated there. Fur seals, and pods of bottlenose and common dolphins frequent the adjacent waters.

White Island or Whakaari lies around 50 kilometres out to sea from Whakatane, largely a steaming crater rising only 321 metres above the sea. The bulk of the volcano (70 percent) is underwater and its crater nearly so. On a still day the plume of steam and gas can rise 10 kilometres, visible from the top of Mt Tarawera some 100 kilometres away.

Whakaari is a seabird island. Maori used it to harvest grey-faced petrel, which burrows into the outer walls of the volcano. From spring to autumn, Australian gannets nest on a headland close to the island's landing place.

Going ashore on Whakaari involves stepping straight into the steaming cauldron of its crater. The landscape is continually swept by clouds of steam and the air is fouled with the acidic stink of sulphur. The earth shudders underfoot as subterranean forces threaten to break through the hot springs and fumaroles. Yellow sheets and crusts of sulphur edge the ever-shifting path around the crater lakes. Rearing overhead, the steep inner walls of the volcano are fissured with steam vents. Slips show how the walls fall unpredictably, burying the steaming floor of the crater, thus building up pressure for an eruption. This is both the largest and the most active of the New Zealand volcanoes.

Whakaari has been intermittently mined for its sulphur in several attempts between 1885 and 1933. In September

1914 the collapse of a crater wall swept the mine and its workers away in a lahar, killing all 12 men. The ruins of the last mine, built in the 1920s, are buried in ash and coated with corrosion.

The arc of volcanoes marking the edge of the Pacific continental plate ends offshore in a chain of subterranean volcanoes. These mark the subduction zone where the Pacific Plate is diving under the Indo-Australian Plate. The northernmost of these submarine volcanoes is called Whakatane but it is preceded by the Rumbles, a series of vents on the sea floor, named for the fact that they were first detected by acoustic soundings underwater.

Beyond this Taupo volcanic arc lies the Kermadec arc and in turn the Tongan arc. With the exception of the Kermadec Island volcanoes, 1000 kilometres north of Auckland, the volcanoes of the Kermadec arc are all submarine, further markers of the earth's weakness around the shores of the Pacific Ring of Fire.

▲ TOP: Visiting parties must wear hard hats and breathing masks in case of a sudden discharge of gas from the volcano.

▲ ABOVE: Ruins of an attempt to mine sulphur from Whakaari (White Island) in the 1920s and early 1930s. The acid atmosphere has corroded the remains.

EAST CAPE

EAST CAPE

The coastal road round East Cape offers spectacular seascapes and isolated Maori villages but the rugged hinterland is not easy to explore. The North Island main divide ends here in the Raukumara and Pukeamaru Ranges, their fringes generally entered only by local hunters in search of pig and deer.

State Highway 2 runs on from Whakatane in the eastern Bay of Plenty to Opotiki, where there is a notable puriri tree in the Hikutaia domain. The tree, Taketakerau, spreads over 27 metres and its five trunks enclose hollows where Maori once buried their ancestors. The domain itself has only native trees, and is regarded as one of the best collections in New Zealand.

At Opotiki SH2 heads south, taking a winding and often forested route to Gisborne through the Raukumara Range. The Coastal Pacific Highway, SH36, however, follows the sea coast round East Cape for 333 kilometres to Gisborne. Rivers that rise in the Raukumara mountains run in steep gorges and debouch along the coast as raging torrents. Beaches become covered by the bones of ancient trees swept down by the floods. Small farms straggle along the patches of flat land.

The East Cape is largely a Maori district, and the carved meeting houses are still in use. In contrast to the rest of New Zealand, life continues along traditional lines, much as it was 50 years ago. On the roads one often passes local people riding horses. The old dairy factories and meatworks are abandoned, however. The development of modern land transport has led to the gradual decay of the old deepwater wharves which served as places to load coastal vessels.

Te Kaha was once a village of 'bay whalers'. Into the 1920s, local Maori put out to sea in rowboats when migrating whales were seen offshore. These they harpooned from their whaleboats and dragged inshore for processing.

Whangaparaoa, further on, means 'bay of whales' and it is the place where two major migratory canoes of the Maori fetched up. One tradition tells of an argument between them over ownership of a dead whale.

▶ *PAGES 106–107 AND OPPOSITE, TOP: Lonely ocean beaches are a feature of the East Cape region.*

▶ *OPPOSITE, BOTTOM LEFT: Maori carved meeting houses are private places but are often seen from the road. This one, Whitireia at Whangara, recalls the tradition of the whalerider Paikea and was the setting of the movie* Whale Rider. *The village is closed to the public.*

▶ *OPPOSITE, BOTTOM RIGHT: Looking toward the East Cape which can be reached by a long coastal side road from SH35.*

▲ ABOVE: *The remains of old wharves stretching out to deeper water are signs of the days when coastal steamers were the main communication route. Produce, particularly wool, was floated off from bullock carts or wheeled out from now abandoned onshore stores. Local Maori value traditional fisheries, including shellfish, on these coasts.*

Both Tainui (Waikato) and Arawa (Bay of Plenty) canoes approached these shores perhaps 800 years ago when the coastal pohutukawa were in full bloom. Seeing the proliferation of red blossoms those aboard the Tainui canoe threw away their sacred garlands of red, only to find the replacement pohutukawa blooms did not last.

At Te Araroa what is claimed to be the largest pohutukawa in New Zealand sprawls at the school gate. The tree, known as Te Waha o Rerekohu, has 22 branches, nearly all rising from ground level. It is thought to be around 300 years old, and named 'the mouth of Rerekohu' after a contemporary chief who gathered tributes of food in a storehouse under its branches.

In many places manuka shrubland now covers abandoned farmland. The manuka *Leptospermum scoparium* that grows along this coast is believed to contain a special essential oil. A traditional medicine, it is now harvested and sold as an antimicrobial oil — antibacterial, antifungal and insecticidal. Honey made from the same shrub has similar qualities.

The journey south from the Cape runs inland, crossing more rivers from the Raukumara Range with occasional twists to seaside settlements. At Tikitiki it meets the Waiapu River, a shingle-skeined riverbed which drains the east of the Raukumara Ranges.

Along this road are the best views of Mt Hikurangi, claimed to be the first place in New Zealand to see the light. (The international dateline deviates to the west to take in the other claimant, the Chatham Islands, 400 miles eastward into the Pacific.)

Hikurangi is the sacred mountain of the Ngati Porou people. At 1752 metres it is the highest non-volcanic peak in the North Island. Its neighbours, Whanokao (1625 metres), Aorangi (1272 metres), Wharekia (965 metres) and Taitai (677 metres), are sometimes called the Waiapu Mountains but are actually the core of the Raukumara Range at the northern end of the North Island main divide.

Ruatoria is an inland town where SH35 crosses the Waiapu River before continuing south through Te Puia Springs (hot pools) to coastal Tokomaru Bay, Tolaga Bay, and on to Gisborne, the regional capital of the Eastland country. It was here that James Cook made his first landfall in New Zealand, later calling at a number of bays on his circumnavigation northward. He called the Gisborne coast

INTRODUCED TREES

The Eastwoodhill Arboretum at Ngatapa, 35 kilometres inland from Gisborne, is devoted to introduced trees. Its founder, William Douglas Cook, began planting on his hill farm in 1910. Covering some 135 hectares, Eastwoodhill contains more than 3500 taxa — species, subspecies and varieties — among its 30,000 specimens. It is said to be the largest collection of northern hemisphere trees in the southern hemisphere.

Douglas Cook was driven by fears that nuclear war could rob Europe of its native plants and saw Eastwoodhill as a place to store their gene pools. It is regarded by arboriculturists as the national arboretum of New Zealand and has an associated herbarium and educational centre. Incidentally, when Cook found the soil unsuitable for rhododendrons he and others established another national collection, the Pukeiti Rhododendron Trust, on the slopes of Mt Egmont/Taranaki (page 153).

▲ *ABOVE: 'Freedom camping' attracts holidaymakers but most settlements have camping grounds.*

▲ *ABOVE: The Waioeka Gorge is a direct route through the Raukumara Ranges from Opotiki to Gisborne but it bypasses the East Cape.*

THE CURSE OF EROSION

The East Coast region is reputed to be losing 10 times the amount of soil lost through erosion anywhere else on earth. Pioneer farmers cleared the steep forests and the newly exposed mudstones started to move. In a great storm in 1988, Cyclone Bola, the hills slipped under the impact of more than half a metre of rain in just 72 hours. (Some claim up to a metre fell in places.) Efforts to rebuild the land include extensive commercial forestry but it could take 100 years or more to scour the accumulated debris from the riverbeds.

Poverty Bay because he could get no food or help from local Maori.

The region inland is badly damaged by erosion. Cloudbursts on bared land led to sudden and massive floods. The mudstone hills have been stripped of soil.

One spectacular slip is still moving since the land beneath it melted into mud in 1915. This Tarndale Slip, inland from Gisborne, covers 50 hectares and is eroding back into the Mangatu Slip on the other side of the mountain.

The bed of the Waipaoa River has been raised some 30 metres with spoil from the eroding hills and now threatens to overtop the flood banks built along its fertile riverflats.

Gisborne's flat lands are now a centre of the wine industry, with a reputation for making the best of New Zealand chardonnays.

▶ *OPPOSITE: Hikurangi (1754 metres) is the sacred mountain of the Ngati Porou people. It is claimed to be the first place in New Zealand to see the light of morning. Hikurangi stands in the rugged Raukumara Ranges, visible from SH36 between Tikitiki and Te Puia Springs.*

HAWKE'S BAY/
WAIRARAPA

H A W K E ' S   B A Y /
W A I R A R A P A

The east coast of the North Island is a dry area in the shadow of the island's main divide. These extremely rugged mountains, heavily forested and not to be tackled by the inexperienced, run from the Rimutaka Range east of Wellington to the hinterland of East Cape. Each section carries its own geographic name but effectively the series of mountain ranges divides off the east coast as a distinctive part of the North Island.

The way in across the ranges is often wild but the country running eastward to the sea is generally bland.

Lake Tutira, 30 kilometres north from Napier on SH2, provides a visual oasis among the desiccated hills of inland Hawke's Bay. The lake is known for its waterfowl, including Australian coot and dabchick. Ringed with exotic willows, the lake shores are the subject of a replanting programme to restore native cover.

Lake Tutira was set aside as a wildlife reserve in the 1920s by its pioneer owner, the farmer and naturalist W.H. Guthrie-Smith. In his massive tome *Tutira: The Story of a New Zealand Sheep Station*, Guthrie-Smith writes of the countryside's human and natural history from Maori times, dealing in finicking detail with every natural event on his farm from purchase in 1882 till 1921. The book is still in print in the United States and is regarded as a classic of conservation.

In the worked-over hills of inland Hawke's Bay, the Department of Conservation and many volunteers have established one of DoC's 'mainland islands', protecting plants and wildlife from predators. Boundary Stream is accessible from Lake Tutira by turning into Pohokura Road, running to the eastern slopes of the Maungaharuru Range.

Boundary Stream 'island' is surrounded by farmed hills, and protects 800 hectares of forest, some of it formerly logged, and rising to montane areas. Wet cliffs overhang regenerating forests and deep gorges. The initial task of eradicating the many pests, such as possums, rats, cats, mustelids and goats, was accomplished in the 1990s.

◀ *OPPOSITE: Heavily layered cliffs approaching Cape Kidnappers are made of uplifted marine beds and successive pumice showers. The coastline is followed by people wanting to see the gannets which nest on the rocks and stacks beneath the cliffs.*

◀ *PAGES 114–115: Clifftop gannet colony on Cape Kidnappers.*

▲ *ABOVE: The shores of Lake Tutira are being replanted with native species. Turn off here to see Boundary Stream Mainland Island.*

BLACK-FRONTED DOTTEREL

The shingle riverbeds of Hawke's Bay provide habitat for the unusual black-fronted dotterel. This Australian bird established itself as a native during the 1950s and the bulk of its population can still be found here. Its short red beak, and the V-shaped black pattern on its chest and through its eye, distinguish the bird from the native banded dotterel. Populations have since spread to riverbeds from Manawatu southwards; look for them on smaller shingle riverbeds in the South Island too.

The recovery of the forest requires continual pest control but the results have been rewarding. Brown kiwi and bush robin have been released again; saddleback (tieke) and kokako have also been introduced. Flocks of up to 30 native pigeons have been reported. New Zealand falcon hunt over the treetops.

A complementary creche where young kiwi can be raised to adulthood in a protected environment has been established by ring-fencing 40 hectares around nearby Lake Opouahi.

The lower country of Hawke's Bay and the Wairarapa tends to lower hills and broader plains. The mountain rivers spread from their gorges to spill over broadening shingle riverbeds, with occasional wetlands close to the sea. Look at the riverbeds to see wading birds, including black-fronted dotterels which breed on the shingle in summer.

Horrific earthquakes wrecked much of

the cities of Napier and Hastings in 1931. At that time, the vast Ahuriri Lagoon behind Napier's Bluff Hill was lifted up some 2 metres, creating 3600 hectares of new land.

The remnants of the Ahuriri Lagoon stretch as far as Napier Airport and are a locally vaunted place for viewing unusual waterbirds, including waders from the northern hemisphere. Unfortunately uncontrolled dogs also frequent the tidal flats.

The real natural appeal of the Napier district is contained in the Cape Kidnappers gannet colony (October–April). Competing concessions operate: one winds out through a luxury golf course and ends right alongside the gannets which nest on the clifftop. There is another colony in view further down the dramatically falling headland.

The alternative tour follows the rocky beach below the giant cliffs of the Cape. These cliffs are layered in alternate bands of submarine sands and volcanic deposits,

AXIAL MOUNTAINS

The series of axial mountain ranges which separate the east coast of the North Island from the rest begins at Wellington and ends near East Cape. While each bears its own name the ranges are practically continuous, sometimes with related front ranges on the east coast side. The mountains begin across the harbour from Wellington as the Rimutaka Range and proceed north as the Tararua Range. The Ruahine Range runs north from the Manawatu Gorge, becoming the Kaweka Range behind Napier, then comes the tangle of the Ahimanawa and Kaimanawa ranges and Te Urewera, inland from Gisborne, and finally the Raukumara Range running north toward East Cape.

▼ *BELOW: Gannets at Cape Kidnappers; some feeding chicks.*

▲ TOP AND ABOVE: *The North Island kaka is established in Pukaha/Mount Bruce Wildlife Reserve. Introduced to the forest in 1996, the free-ranging birds get supplementary food each afternoon.*

THE NAPIER EARTHQUAKE

The Napier earthquake registered 7.9 on the Richter scale. It devastated the city, killing 161 people. Fire then roared through several blocks of the ruins. In Hastings, 21 kilometres south, 93 died and there were more fires. In the ensuing two or three years both business districts were substantially rebuilt; Napier notably in Art Deco style and Hastings in Spanish Mission.

creating a spectacular edge to the land (and a good place to look about for fossils). Gannets nest here about the bottom of the cliffs and on offshore rock stacks.

The Wairarapa country, south of Napier, extends over plains and low hills to the southern tip of the North Island at Cape Palliser. For nature-lovers, the most outstanding site is the Pukaha/Mt Bruce Wildlife Reserve. Begun by a farmer who fenced off his forest and experimented with ways to raise the takahe, the reserve is now run by the Department of Conservation as its centre for rare and endangered species. There are a few huge flight aviaries sheltered within the canopy of the forest itself, containing kaka (the bush parrot), kokako, saddleback, kiwi, and both red- and yellow-crowned parakeets (kakariki). Living wild in some 1000 hectares of bush are healthy populations of native pigeon (kereru), kaka, kakariki, kiwi and some takahe. Kaka were introduced in 1996–7 and have populated the forest. Tui and bellbird add to the chorus of birdsong. Flocks of free-flying kaka and giant eels are fed each afternoon.

South of here the Wairarapa valleys become more separated from the sea. While the Wairarapa boasts of its wild beaches they are a long way off the beaten track of SH2, through low-lying hills.

Castlepoint, 65 kilometres from Masterton, is locally popular, with its geographical 'castle', named by Captain Cook, and a lighthouse. Sometimes dolphins may be seen, while fur seals also haul out here.

In the southern reaches of the region two lakes are well known for their wetland birds. Lake Wairarapa is rumoured to be so shallow in parts that some claim to

have walked across it in drought times. Lake Onoke lies at the southernmost point of the North Island, protected from the sea by a shingle bank. Among the 100 or so different bird species recorded here, over a 10-year period, are several northern waders including golden plover, Japanese snipe, eastern bar-tailed godwit and lesser knot.

▲ *ABOVE: The native forest on Mount Bruce extends over 1000 hectares. While some rare birds are held in flight aviaries, within the forest, growing numbers of species such as kaka fly free.*

CENTRAL PLATEAU

TAUPO

Lake Taupo occupies the craters of a vast volcano which last erupted, with devastating impact, less than 2000 years ago. Scientists and historians have argued over the possible date, finding in the writings of classic Romans and Chinese various descriptions of a vast eruption which darkened the skies as far as the northern hemisphere. The Taupo eruption, originally dated from these historic records at 186 CE, showered the centre of the North Island with vast deposits of volcanic tephra, burying and reshaping the landscape. (232 CE is now the favoured date.)

Because of the scale of this volcano, the name Taupo has been given to the whole volcanic zone which begins to the south, with Ruapehu in Tongariro National Park, and passes through the lake to Rotorua and out to sea to White Island and beyond.

Taupo is said to be the 'most productive' volcano in the world, in terms of frequency of eruption and the quantity of material ejected. Its massive eruption 1800-odd years ago produced 110 cubic kilometres of rock and ash, some of which is estimated to have risen 50 kilometres into the sky.

As a result of Taupo eruptions, the Waikato River has from time to time clogged and changed course, sometimes flowing out to the east coast by way of the Hauraki Plains, and otherwise taking its present course to the west coast, or through the Manukau Harbour in Auckland.

Thermal activity at Taupo is presently limited to local areas.

Approaching Taupo from the Waikato by SH1, there is signposted access by a side road to an extensive thermal field

▲ *ABOVE: Steaming hot springs and sinter terraces at Orakei Korako.*

◀ *OPPOSITE: Motutaiko, a volcanic island in Lake Taupo, is a protected Maori burial ground.*

◀ *PAGES 122–123: Winter snow buries the subalpine slopes of Mount Ruapehu with the cone of Ngauruhoe and Tongariro beyond.*

called Orakei Korako, on the banks of the Waikato River. Once it was famous for its geysers but these were flooded when the Waikato River was dammed at Ohakuri in 1961. It is still a major attraction, approached by boat across the river.

A steaming field of mudpools and hot springs, with spectacular sinter terraces, rises up the hillside above the river. The Emerald Terrace, over which hot water runs at up to 60°C, is coloured white and golden; brightest where the water is hottest, fading to browns and greens where it is not so hot. The Golden Fleece Terrace is 5 metres high and 40 metres long. A delicate white and cream sinter mound supports the sparkling Diamond Geyser. There are more than 120 blue chloride pools among the phenomena in the multicoloured crater called the Artist's Palette.

The road from Rotorua to Taupo, SH5, runs across the down-faulted plain of

▼ BELOW: *The long view of Taupo Moana is closed by mountains of the Tongariro National Park in the far distance.*

Broadlands, where steam and pipes in the fields mark out where deep drills have tapped superheated steam to generate electricity. On the western hills above, the Ohaaki power station is a landmark.

The two routes to Taupo, SH1 and SH5, merge at Wairakei, once the most active of the geothermal fields. Giant geysers and other thermal wonders were lost when their fields were tapped for electricity generation in 1958. Around 100 wells tap superheated steam between 600 and 1200 metres underground, to produce up to 192 megawatts of power. The pipes that feed the turbines are a prominent roadside feature where signs warn the motorist about the drifting clouds of steam.

The Craters of the Moon are the most spectacular remains of geothermal activity in the area. Just west of SH1, they comprise fields of boiling mud, fumaroles and a fitful geyser. The areas fringing the hot pools are clad in bright green plants, prostrate manuka, mosses and fern allies, flourishing in the overheated soil.

Taupo town itself sits by the outlet of the Waikato River and there is some evidence along its gorge of more mudpools and steam vents. The Armed Constabulary established camp there in the 1860s and the modern complex of thermal baths is still known as the AC baths. The bulk of the volcano Tauhara rises on the eastern edge of town. There are further signs of vulcanism in the distant panorama of Tongariro National Park, more than 50 kilometres south beyond the lake.

The name Taupo Moana likens the lake to a sea, a fitting description for New Zealand's largest lake, which spreads over 619 square kilometres. The huge volcanic eruptions which formed it began around 300,000 years ago. The present lake was shaped about 10,500 years ago, when basins of magma underground were drained by eruptions and the roof fell in, to form the caldera now occupied by its waters.

The last eruption, some 1800 years ago, was from an underwater vent that still bubbles. The dome of Motutaiko Island is volcanic as are several other hills surrounding the shores of the lake. White cliffs are formed from ignimbrite ejected in the eruptions.

The route around the eastern shore of Taupo, SH1, passes through small Maori villages and holiday settlements. Layers of earth visible in road cuttings and erosion patterns show how this landscape has been shaped from the ignimbrite and pumice eruptions of Taupo. The highway reveals a number of interesting natural features, including cliffs of volcanic ignimbrite, wetlands, streams and some wilder shores of the lake where native birds shelter.

The waters of Lake Taupo are frequented by several native duck species, black swan, coot, pukeko, herons and shags which may be seen drying themselves on shoreline rocks. The road off SH1 at Turangi, on the famed trout fishery of Tongariro, crosses the outlet of the Tongariro power scheme at Tokaanu. Tunnels carry the waters of tributaries of rivers as distant as the Whanganui through the mountains.

Beyond Tokaanu, on the southern shore of the lake, the road passes through dense swamps of flax and raupo (bulrushes). Narrow side roads run to the lake through the homes of bittern, and fernbirds. These sparrow-sized birds with long, ragged

▲ ABOVE: *The young Waikato River is forced into a 15-metre wide gorge above the Huka Falls, just north of Taupo town.*

tails may be seen clambering up the reeds to call to others hidden in the swamp.

There are hot springs and other thermal phenomena among the manuka trees about Tokaanu. The bulk of Kakaramea, which rises above the southwestern shore, is often seen to steam from a thermal field above the lake. In 1846 it precipitated a huge landslide which buried the Maori village of Te Rapa, killing among others the paramount chief of the Tuwharetoa tribe, Mananui, Te Heuheu Tukino II.

It is possible, but not worthwhile from a wildlife point of view, to travel around the lake by way of the West Taupo Access Road, SH32. This was developed in the 1960s to open up newly developed farmlands but it does not give access to the lake or even a view of it. There is access from it to the rainforests of Pureora Forest Park, however, to the west.

It is possible instead to cross from Tokaanu to the King Country near

Taumarunui by SH41, via the end of the Hauhangaroa Range, a journey notable for the sight of huge native podocarp trees rising above the roadside.

The more usual route to the national park (SH47 from Tokaanu) climbs over the Ponanga Saddle between Pihanga and Kakaramea, both northern outliers of Tongariro National Park. These mountains are also clad in a notable forest of giant totara, rimu and kahikatea. An exquisite little lake, Rotopounamu, lies in a punchbowl of forest in the side of Pihanga. A walk of 1.6 kilometres from the carpark encircles the lake which is as green as the greenstone it is named for. Among the many bush birds look for tiny riflemen, the thumb-sized birds which feed up the mossy trunks of the trees, announcing their presence by a swift *zweet, zweet* call.

The road then passes Rotoaira, and extensive plantings of exotic pines, en route for the main body of Tongariro National Park centred on Whakapapa.

▲ TOP: *Tall podocarps grow on the Ponanga Saddle over Mt Pihanga.*

▲ ABOVE AND OPPOSITE: *A geyser plays at Craters of the Moon, just north of Taupo. The area extends over fields of volcanic mud with vigorous fumaroles and mudpools.*

WAIRAKEI THERMAL FIELD

On Wairakei Road, off SH1 near the service station, there is a viewing area overlooking the geothermal power field. Just south of Wairakei, look also for the visitor displays of the Volcanic Activity Centre, and the spectacle of the gorge above the Huka Falls channelling the Waikato River into a gap barely 15 metres across. The Craters of the Moon lie to the west of the highway, accessed by a signposted road.

THE TONGARIRO
VOLCANOES

The volcanoes of the central North Island comprise a World Heritage Area with an unusual double-listing. The international authority recognises the national park in both its categories: for wilderness features, and also for cultural significance.

New Zealand's first national park was established here in 1894, following the gifting of the Tongariro volcanic peaks by the paramount chief of the Tuwharetoa people, Horonuku, Te Heuheu Tukino IV.

At that time, it was only the third national park in the world, and protected just 2630 hectares of mountaintops considered sacred by Maori. The park has since grown to surround the volcanoes, and includes the bush-clad outliers of Pihanga and Kakaramea on the southern shores of Lake Taupo, 75,259 hectares in all.

The volcanoes of Tongariro National Park are still active. They are also readily accessible with three roads climbing to the snowline on Mt Ruapehu, and an extensive system of short and long tracks throughout the park. Ruapehu at 2797 metres is the highest mountain in the North Island and the southernmost in the Tongariro volcanic zone.

The lower slopes of the park are clad in red tussock and thickets of dracophyllum and other whipcord shrubs. Introduced Scottish heather has invaded this damp area, often taking the place of native hebes, orchids and other wildflowers. The usually secretive fernbird flourishes in this open country, particularly in the vicinity of the Skotel at Whakapapa where birds call to each other from the top of shrubs along the track.

Forests are restricted to the western slopes of Ruapehu where there is more rain. Beech forest rises to the subalpine shrubs at which level the mountain cedar pahautea may stand sentinel.

There is rainforest too in the vicinity of Ohakune but much of the original cover has been damaged by volcanic activity and by timber-millers who worked here before the national park was extended.

The sliver of forest on Tongariro is dominated by Hall's totara rising up a ridge to the tussock country.

Two of the ski access roads on Ruapehu

◀ *OPPOSITE: Evening view of Mt Ruapehu in eruption in 1996. The erupting steam carried ash up to 10 kilometres into the air before drifting off in a descending cloud over the nearby King Country.*

Bogs and swamps are a feature of the countryside surrounding the wetter, western margins of the mountains. Native flax flourishes in wetlands in the vicinity of National Park village.

are steep and rough but the road from Whakapapa to Iwikau Village on the snowline is well formed and sealed. Parking areas off this road serve local walks and give an opportunity to examine the changing nature of the mountainside. Alpine scrublands occur above the beech and tussock, usually between 1100 and 1600 metres. The unusual pipit is common here, picking insects among the rocks.

The tiniest of New Zealand trees, the snow totara, grows here, just a few centimetres high. It can be identified as a member of the group of giant podocarp pines by its fleshy-footed seeds. Its relatives grow elsewhere as the largest trees in the rainforest.

In summer when the snowfields shrink, the subalpine zone reveals a rich variety of flowering plants, including hairy-leaved daisies and shiny-leaved buttercups, little hebes, and whipcords of dracophyllum, on rocks set about with mosses and lichens. Alpine moss and herbfields occur between 1500 and 2000 metres.

Ski-lifts on the Whakapapa slopes operate in summer, giving access over the volcanic rockfields to the upper mountain. This area requires caution as mountain weather can be suddenly variable, requiring warm, weatherproof clothing and some knowledge of survival techniques. In summer, guided walks may be available to the mountaintop.

The warm crater lake of Ruapehu is evidence of its continued activity. Sulphurous waters bubble in the active throat of the volcano, rising occasionally to spill over and rush down the mountainside in a mass of ash and melted snow.

In 1969 such a lahar swept down the Whakapapa skifield shortly after 2000 skiers had left the field for the day. An overflow on Christmas Eve 1953 had tragic consequences when a lahar tore down the Whangaehu River and swept away a bridge pile just before the night express rushed over. The locomotive and five carriages plunged into the river killing 151 of those aboard.

Ruapehu has erupted several times in the past 50 years: in 1945–6, then several times in the latter 1960s, again in 1971, 1975, 1978, 1979, and spectacularly (as illustrated) in 1995 and 1996.

THE TONGARIRO ALPINE CROSSING

Across the tussock grassland from Ruapehu, Tongariro (1967 metres) is a large and complex volcano with several craters and centres of thermal activity. The near-perfect cone of Ngauruhoe (2291 metres) at the southern end of the

TRACK TRANSPORT

Road-end carparks in remote places are known to be insecure. Fortunately, a number of bus services from National Park village and from park headquarters at Whakapapa access both ends of the Tongariro Crossing in summer.

▼ BELOW: The Blue Lakes on the top of Mt Tongariro lie in explosion craters. The view is from the rim of the active Red Crater.

▲ *ABOVE: Climbing the ridge above the Red Crater on the Tongariro Crossing.*

THE DESERT ROAD

The Rangipo (formerly Onetapu) Desert is the result of poor soils and harsh conditions rather than lack of rain. Lying to the east of the volcanoes, it is bordered by the Desert Road, the sector of SH1 linking Turangi on Lake Taupo with the SH49 junction at Waiouru. Clumps of tussock shelter a few wildflowers in summer but the drying winds have created extensive areas of bare volcanic sand between the highway and the mountains. In winter it freezes under snow, with ground frosts on 100 days a year. This area was once beech forest, flattened and burnt by the last Taupo eruption. In places, skeletons of the old forest lie exposed on the desert sand.

mountain is simply the youngest of its vents, and the most active.

Maori believed the volcanoes of Aotearoa began here. When Ngatoro-i-rangi, navigator of the Arawa migration, moved inland from the Bay of Plenty, he decided to climb the mountain with his slave Auruhoe. Storm conditions overcame them and Ngatoro-i-rangi called on his sisters in the ancestral homeland of Hawaiki to send fire to warm them. The fire came overland, its sparks igniting thermal activity along the way at places such as White Island/Whakaari, Rotorua, Tarawera, Orakei Korako and Taupo. Unfortunately, the fire was too late for Auruhoe, whom Ngatoro-i-rangi threw into the erupting crater of the mountain as a sacrifice of thanks.

Ngauruhoe is continually active, its eruption detectable at its lowest level as a wisp of steam and gas rising from the cone. From time to time the mountain

▲ *ABOVE: Snow emphasises the younger cone of Ngauruhoe, most active of the Tongariro volcanoes.*

is more violent, spewing forth clouds of steam and gas, and sometimes spilling lava or throwing out blocks and cinders. Red-hot lava flowed down its flanks during the eruptions of 1870, 1949 and 1954. Eruptions in the early 1970s produced ash clouds from 2 to 12 kilometres high, and scattered huge blocks of volcanic basalt on the mountain's flanks.

A walk across the volcanoes of adjacent Tongariro has been claimed as the world's greatest one-day walk. A road leads from SH47 to near the foot of Ngauruhoe, and a track leads from there to the head of the Mangatepopo Valley between Ngauruhoe and the rest of Mt Tongariro. From the saddle, the famous Tongariro Crossing heads across the craters of the volcanic complex. Like a molar, the top of Tongariro is a complex of ridges and craters, several occupied by lakes or sheets of volcanic sand.

The Tongariro Crossing is a 19.4 kilometre high-level walk across this volcanic landscape. South and Central craters are flat areas, possibly created by

WORLD HERITAGE AREAS

New Zealand has three world heritage listings under UNESCO, the United Nations Educational, Scientific and Cultural Organization. The system recognises internationally more than 800 significant sites in the world, either natural (the Grand Canyon) or cultural (the Pyramids). The natural sites in New Zealand include Te Wahi Pounamu-South West New Zealand (page 268) and the subantarctic island groups including Campbell, Auckland, Antipodes, Bounty and the Snares. Tongariro is the only world heritage area in New Zealand to be doubly recognised: for its natural features, and for its Maori cultural history.

glaciers in the last ice age, and now filled with volcanic ash. A ridge above the Red Crater overlooks an active volcanic landscape where steam is constantly rising from fissures in the crater wall. Green and blue lakes mark explosion craters. The walk continues through tussock fields down to the Ketetahi Hut and a view of the steam clouds from Ketetahi Springs, a Maori reserve. The descent then winds through mixed forests dominated by Hall's totara to a parking lot off SH46.

SHORT WALKS

A number of exciting walks radiate from park headquarters at Whakapapa, extending from 1–2 hours to a five-day trek around the mountains. Short walks across tussock grassland and through low beech forest lead to volcanic lahars, the Taranaki Falls, wild streams which may have rare blue duck or whio, and the colourful Silica Springs. Longer walks cross the summits of the Tongariro volcanoes, or climb to the craters of the Ngauruhoe or Ruapehu volcanoes — when conditions are suitable.

◀ TOP: The Rangipo Desert stretches from SH1 to the foot of Mt Ruapehu. Parts of it are bare sand.

◀ ABOVE LEFT: Endangered blue duck, a torrent dweller, survives on wilder streams such as the Whakapapa.

◀ LEFT: Silica Springs are an hour's walk from Whakapapa Village, through silver beech forest and across tussock country. The waters of the springs have deposited cream-coloured silica brought from underground in suspension. The orange and brown colours are algal growths which stain the growing deposits.

▲ TOP: *The Ketetahi Springs on the northern side of Tongariro are sacred to Maori and closed to visitors.*

▲ ABOVE: *Several peaks surround the 17-hectare crater lake on Mt Ruapehu. When it overflows, lahars of mud and ash can sweep down the mountainside and over the countryside below.*

WAIKATO/
KING COUNTRY

WAIKATO / KING COUNTRY

▲ *ABOVE: A stand of kahikatea, or white pine, surviving on the floor of the Waikato Valley. They favour damp land.*

◀ *PAGES 138–139: Mt Pirongia viewed from the Waipa Valley, Waikato.*

The Waikato River is one of the great natural features of New Zealand yet it runs now largely through farmland and plantation forest. From time to time its course is disrupted by giant hydro-electricity dams and their long, deep lakes. Born as the Tongariro River, on the southeastern slopes of Ruapehu and skirting the Tongariro volcanoes, the Waikato flows through Lake Taupo and out to the Tasman Sea near Auckland. This makes it the country's longest river at 425 kilometres.

Over the millennia, this 'flowing water' has shaped the land. At times the Waikato has flowed to the east coast through a distinctive rift near Karapiro and down to the Firth of Thames via the Hauraki Plains. Its latest shift, to flow to the west again, occurred about 19,000 years ago when volcanic silt from an eruption upstream blocked the Hinuera Gorge and redirected the river's flow down its present valleys.

In its lower reaches the Waikato flows through a broad valley once a place of tall kahikatea trees and extensive swamps. Water from the adjacent hills is in places ponded behind barriers of volcanic ash brought into the valley by the ancestral Waikato. Vegetation caught in such places has built up deep layers of peat over the

▲ ABOVE: *Complex river control spreads the floodwaters of the Waikato into ponding areas and natural lakes.*

millennia. Such peat swamps and lakes still lie visible to the sides of the river. These are the haunt of many waterbirds. The lakes are shallow, some only 3 metres deep, and threatened by eutrophication from farming on adjacent land.

A shrub forest of willow, manuka, flax and reed species surrounds some lakes, but access to the water is limited to a broad view of the wetland expanse from high points along the road. Wet fields along the main highway may reveal cattle egret in winter, white-faced heron, spur-winged plover, and various ducks. Flocks of hundreds of black swans provide a management problem for farmers around the lakes where pastures are eaten and fouled by excess numbers of this Australian game bird.

Centuries ago, Maori cleared a lot of the lowland valleys of the Waipa and the Waikato by burning. Farming and timber-milling since the beginning of European settlement have virtually destroyed the wilderness aspect of these valleys. Only occasional tall clumps of kahikatea along a streambed are a reminder of what might have been.

Ships no longer brave the bar at Port Waikato. Volcanic sands and the product of upstream erosion have made the river entrance shallow and dangerous. From this point south it is difficult to approach the wild Waikato coast. Long beaches of black sand run south to Taranaki, carried there by longshore drift from ancient volcanoes. Their product, titanomagnetite, popularly known as ironsand, is used for making steel at Waiuku and in Japan.

NEW ZEALAND WETLANDS CENTRE

The settlement of Rangiriri, just off SH1, is the headquarters of the New Zealand Wetlands Centre. From here, a circular route can be followed around two of the peat lakes.

The traveller south must decide at Hamilton whether to make a journey by SH1 toward Taupo, or Rotorua, or to follow the course of the Waipa River which flows from the King Country. It is this latter journey by SH3 which leads into the wilds of the Waikato west coast (and ultimately a choice of visiting Taranaki or Tongariro). Roads from the Waipa Valley access three broad harbours along this otherwise bleak coast.

The famous surf breaks at Raglan roll onto black sand beaches which protect a wandering and sheltered harbour. These harbour arms are a breeding ground for fish and a feeding place for birds, especially the migrant waders from the Arctic which visit in summer.

The ancient volcano of Pirongia (959 metres) is a landmark of the journey south, standing between the Waipa Valley and the west coast. Its dense forests are preserved in a conservation park covering 11,748 hectares.

▲ *ABOVE: Sea cliffs at Tongaporutu. Volcanic sands, swept up the west coast of the North Island by long-shore drift, have produced beaches of ironsand stretching 480 kilometres from the Whangaehu River to the Kaipara Harbour. The distinctive black sands are mined, at Waikato north head, to feed the Glenbrook steel mill. In the remote Taharoa area, south of the Kawhia Harbour, ironsand is dredged, separated and fed by pipeline to ships anchored offshore.*

The base of the basalt mountain is 17 kilometres across. Deeply dissected valleys, with tracks accessible from a number of road ends, penetrate the mountains but the country is rugged. Sheer cliffs and forest-covered plateaux complicate its geography which rises to several peaks around 900 metres, including Pirongia's twin, The Cone, at 945 metres.

The western slopes still reflect the original cover of tawa and kohekohe with some rimu. Higher up, the forest includes rimu, miro and Hall's totara, kamahi and rewarewa. An early explorer, the botanist Thomas Cheeseman, wrote of scrambling over the top of a canopy of twisted kamahi and subalpine shrubs to reach the summit; so dense was the structure of the subalpine forest he could not walk through it.

Pirongia is by far the largest in a line of extinct volcanoes. The smaller Karioi (756 metres) stands above the coast south of Raglan. It is possible to follow a complex network of local roads round Karioi heading further south behind the remote Aotea Harbour to Kawhia, but the roads are often narrow, steep and shingled. Main traffic usually flows back from Raglan to the Waipa Valley, skirting around Pirongia with access to Kawhia via Otorohanga (SH31).

Kawhia is the largest of the west coast harbours, an estuary hosting many migrant wading birds in summer. The southernmost mangroves are found here, not much more than ankle height. Saltwater rushes and reeds take their place further south.

Giant dunes enclose both Aotea Harbour and Kawhia, black sand dunes rising to 100 metres or so. On the outer edge of the Kawhia Harbour, Te Puia hot springs bubble up from the beach around the low-tide mark, attracting bathers who scrape out a warm pool in the sand.

The Maori migratory canoe Tainui fetched up at Kawhia after being portaged across the Auckland isthmus and sailing down the Tasman coast. It tied up to one in a line of pohutukawa trees which still overhang the inner harbour. Tainui carried the ancestors of the Tainui and Maniapoto people, who in time spread across the hills to occupy the Waikato

PIRONGIA FOREST PARK

Pirongia Forest Park can be accessed from the ends of several roads which follow the eroded volcanic valleys into the mountain. The rugged terrain protects the remnants of a wider forest which once clothed this region. This is a mixed forest of 11,748 hectares, rich in native hardwood species, with tawa and kohekohe dominant. In other places there are varied clumps of rimu, miro, Hall's totara, kamahi and rewarewa.

▲ *ABOVE: Typical King Country forest. Southern species begin creeping into the forest composition, including the columnar tawa.*

ALTERNATIVE ROUTES

It is possible to avoid main highway traffic (and Hamilton city) by taking the country road along the west bank of the Waikato River. There are bridges across the river at Mercer, Rangiriri, Huntly and Ngaruawahia.

and King Country. Their canoe lies buried by the marae of the Maori village in Kawhia.

The ironsand dunes to the south of Kawhia are pumped to ships standing offshore from the vicinity of Lake Taharoa. This is remote country and most visitors return to Otorohanga before visiting the Waitomo Caves, to the south by SH3, and SH37. The Maori word means 'water running out of a hole'.

Inland again, on SH3, the road offers a choice of destinations at Eight Mile Junction, south of Te Kuiti. State Highway 4 branches off here and heads through the southern King Country via Taumarunui toward Tongariro and Whanganui national parks. The west coast route continues as SH3, climbing through mountains to Taranaki.

At length, SH3 winds down the valley of the Awakino River to a spectacular coast of cliffs and caves in northern Taranaki. The road follows the coast from Awakino to the Mokau River, once a major route inland, and still used by launches.

▲ ABOVE: *The Marakopa Falls on a sideroad from Waitomo west to the coast at Marakopa. Counted with smaller falls just above, the total drop is around 36 metres.*

OTOROHANGA KIWI HOUSE

The Otorohanga Kiwi House and Native Bird Park in the town of Otorohanga provides an opportunity to see rare birds in natural-looking surroundings. Run by the local zoological society, the bird park includes kiwi which are bred there, native parrots and parakeets, and kokako. A broad range of wetland birds includes endangered blue duck and Campbell Island teal. Other displays feature eels, tuatara and 10 species of gecko lizards.

WAITOMO CAVES

The tourist caves are the public face of an extensive formation of limestone, spread over some 25 square kilometres of karst country. The beds of limestone, lying under sandstone and mudstone, are sometimes 150 metres deep.

The main tourist caves are dramatically illuminated and a visit to the Waitomo Cave includes a short trip by boat through an underground passage lit by glow-worms. Stalactites, like stone icicles, hang from the cave ceilings, while stalagmites rise from the floor of the cave to meet them. These structures, and associated encrusted surfaces, are formed as calcium carbonate is slowly deposited from water seeping through the limestone overhead. It is estimated the phenomena of the Waitomo Caves date back 100,000 years.

Visits to wilder caves on adjacent farmland are available through independent cave operators. Known as tomo in Maori, the caves include underground rivers, tunnels, passageways, galleries, squeezes and pot-holes.

Some 85 kilometres of underground passage-ways have been mapped by speleologists in the Waitomo area. Gardiner's Gut alone has more than 12.7 kilometres of passages, and is the sixth-longest cave in New Zealand. Limestone caves have often contained the sub-fossil bones of now-extinct birds, such as moa, which have tumbled in over the millennia.

The limestone country is marked in places by dramatic cliffs and other formations. Some of these bluffs may be the result of collapsed cave systems. The Mangapohue Natural Bridge across a stream off the Marakopa Road is a 15-metre arch created by erosion of a limestone cave.

At Tongaporutu, a short walk along the south bank of the river (when the tide is falling below mid-tide) leads to a deeply dissected cliff face with caves and rock stacks carved by a wild ocean.

From here the cliffs march 10 kilometres southward toward a view of Mt Taranaki on a clear day. At their highest, at Paraninihi (no road access) the cliffs rise 265 metres from the sea. Just offshore, the Paraninihi Marine Reserve protects the Pariokariwa Reef, which has unusual sponge life and soft corals.

The white cliffs are built from the same marine deposits of sandstones and mudstones as Mt Messenger. State Highway 3 winds inland from Tongaporutu over Mt Messenger before reaching the coast again at Urenui in northern Taranaki.

▲ *ABOVE: The entrance to the Aranui cave at Waitomo.*

TARANAKI/
WHANGANUI

TARANAKI

It is possible in inclement weather to drive right round the ring plain of Taranaki without seeing the mountain. Yet its classic cone dominates the landscape when the weather is clear.

Maori say the mountain migrated here from the volcanic plateau of the central North Island. Disappointed in its battle with Tongariro for the love of Pihanga, Taranaki marched away overnight carving out the course of the Whanganui River en route. The mountain was only arrested at dawn by the spreading arms of the Pouakai Range which stopped it disappearing into the sea.

The volcano of Taranaki is the latest in a series of eroded cones spreading south from the shoreline of New Plymouth. The bulk of Taranaki was built about 70,000 years ago though subsequent erosion and eruptions have continued to rebuild it. Pouakai (1399 metres) on its northern edge is estimated to be 250,000 years old, while the Kaitake Range (683 metres) running northward date back about 600,000 years. The Sugar Loaf Islands and Paritutu by New Plymouth are the eroded cores of the earliest volcanoes, estimated at 1,700,000 years old. The surrounding ring plain of rich dairying land is formed by ash spilled from the volcanoes. In places, the flow of this ash has pushed out over the land, taking the form of volcanic lahars, producing gently rolling hillocks and deep-cut streams on the northwest coast in particular.

The current shape of Mt Taranaki was determined only 16,500 years ago, since when erosion has carved deep gullies into the cone, leaving the oldest reefs standing proud of the ridges. Maori likened them to lizard-like monsters, ngarara, declaring the summit to be sacred and therefore out of bounds. The first European explorers, scientist Ernst Dieffenbach and whaler James Heberley, took two days to conquer the peak in 1839. Every time they made a cup of tea they measured the time it took to boil the billy, as a way to calculate the various altitudes they passed through. They calculated the mountain's height to be 2694 metres, a little more than the modern measurement of 2518 metres.

The chances of Taranaki erupting again in the near future are considerable. Fanthams Peak, a parasitic cone on the southern slopes, is the sign of volcanic

◀ OPPOSITE: *Taranaki, a regular volcanic cone of 2518 metres, dominates surrounding farmland. It is deeply eroded, with basalt ridges dissected by steep and rocky gullies.*

◀ PAGES 146–147: *The Whanganui River follows a cliff-bound course through rugged mountains.*

activity breaking out of the mountain some 7000 years ago, and continuing till some 3000 years ago.

There have been seven eruptions on Taranaki in the past 500 years; the historical record laid down in successive ash showers suggests it erupts at least a minor ash shower once a century. The main cone last erupted around 250 years ago, and geologists have warned it is likely to erupt again at any time.

The boundaries of Egmont National Park are most obvious from the air. A dark circlet of forest encloses the mountaintop, reflecting the fact that in 1881 the Taranaki Provincial Council protected all land within six miles (or 9.6 kilometres) of the summit. Farmlands run up to this boundary, showing as a lighter green, to be abruptly capped by dense forest which in turn rises to an often snow-capped peak.

Egmont National Park is named after the English name for the mountain.

The park was created in 1900 from the original forest reserve of 29,292 hectares combined with a further 2400 hectares covering the Pouakai and Kaitake ranges to the north. Subsequently another 1835 hectares have been added.

There are three roads climbing high into the park, taking the visitor to mountain lodges close to the snowline at 900 metres and the network of tracks around and up the mountain.

Driving up from the farmland and into the forest of the national park is curious from a botanical point of view. At first the forests are the typical associations of North Island rainforest; tall trees such as rimu and rata pierce the canopy of hardwoods such as kamahi. Rising higher, however, there are none of the montane beech forests which clothe higher land elsewhere in New Zealand.

It is believed any beech trees were burned off in an eruption which buried the surrounding lowlands. Again, Taranaki was isolated from the rest of the North

▶ OPPOSITE, TOP RIGHT: *The mountain cedar, variously known as kaikawaka or pahautea, is a striking feature of the upper mountain forest (900–1100 metres). Trees rise above the shrubs near the snowline on the eastern flanks of the mountain. The bare skeletons of many have been ascribed to harsh growing conditions, though possums are now known to feed on the growing points of these trees. Some trees are said to be 350–400 years old, surviving the most recent eruptions of Taranaki about 1665 and 1775. Some remnant mountain totara in the upper forest are also believed old enough to have survived these eruptions.*

▶ OPPOSITE, TOP LEFT AND BOTTOM: *Taranaki is notable for the absence of the beech forests which elsewhere form the upper limits of mountain forests. Instead its higher 'goblin' forests are comprised predominantly of many-trunked kamahi hung with mosses and lichens.*

▲ *ABOVE: Viewed from the northeast, the position of Taranaki as one of a series of volcanoes is more apparent. To its right are the remains of the older volcanoes of the Pouakai Range (250,000 years) and the Kaitake Range (600,000 years), both now substantially eroded away. Once they may have stood as high as Taranaki (first erupting only 100,000 years ago). Taranaki itself has been reshaped since then, by further eruptions and the ice ages, removing perhaps some 200 metres from its height.*

◀ *LEFT: 'Leatherwood scrub' comprises the upper band of forest cover on Taranaki. High winds have trimmed the forest of multi-branched tree daisies into a practically impenetrable canopy. At its upper edge, the leatherwood merges with whipcord dracophyllum and tussock which in turn gives way to alpine herbfields, mosses and lichens on the bare rock.*

Island ranges during the ice ages. Because beech mast does not scatter like the seed of many other trees, the beech forests have never regrown on the mountain. Instead of a band of beech at higher altitudes, there is a 'goblin forest' of twisted kamahi hung with mosses and lichens. Above that a dense shrubbery of leathery-leaved tree daisies follows the ridges up to the subalpine zone. Here there is tussock, then herbfields where subalpine flowers, mosses and lichens grow in the ambiguous shelter of lava blocks.

It is a harsh environment overall. At any season, katabatic winds may drop from the mountaintop, sweeping its flanks with cold air and misshaping the treetops. Visitors are warned to carry warm clothing and be prepared for sudden drops in temperature, dense mists and heavy rain; the mountain can be dangerous.

Birdlife on Taranaki is not as rich as in forests elsewhere. The insect life on which many forest birds depend is limited by the harsh mountainous conditions. The absence of lowland forest beyond the park means there is nowhere for the birds to go when winter conditions descend on the mountain. Nevertheless brown kiwi are present, as are robin, pied tit, and the tiny green rifleman which flits up the tree trunks looking for food. High up the mountainside, pipits search for food among the tussocks and herbfields.

The Kaitake Range, to the north of Mt Taranaki/Pouaki, is part of the national park but separated from it. This forest is dominated by tawa, representing the original forest cover of much of the Taranaki lowlands. A road runs over the saddle between the Pouakai and Kaitake ranges past the reserves of the Pukeiti Rhododendron Trust. The only direct road access to the Kaitake Range is on the northern flank, however. Several walking tracks enter the Kaitake forests from side roads off SH45 near Oakura, in particular from Lucy's Gully.

The underwater volcanic remnants of the Sugar Loaf Islands off New Plymouth are protected in a marine reserve. The meeting of cold and warm sea currents makes the waters of this ancient crater particularly rich in fish and other species. Kingfish school here, along with butterfly perch, while fish of both warm and cool seas mix together. Marine creatures include coral, sea anemones, sea cucumbers and red lampshells, primitive brachiopods which look like a damaged thumbnail and are survivors from millions of years ago.

EGMONT OR TARANAKI?

Taranaki is also known as Mt Egmont, the name given by Lieutenant James Cook in 1770 to honour a former First Lord of the British Admiralty. The name Taranaki was later given to the province but the traditional name was not restored to the mountain till 1986. The national park is still named after Egmont.

WHANGANUI

Between Tongariro National Park and the open fields of Taranaki lies a huge tract of broken country, much of it in ancient forest. Crowding trees stand high above the deep gorges of New Zealand's second-longest river, the Whanganui, and along its twisting tributaries.

Beginning with the snow-melt of the Tongariro volcanoes, the Whanganui winds to the Tasman sea coast over 329 kilometres. The milk-chocolate waters are the product of continual erosion in the soft papa country: sandstone and mudstones uplifted around a million years ago from under the sea. Erosion here produces high ridges, unstable slopes and deep gorges.

Maori believe the river gorges were carved by the disgruntled volcano Taranaki escaping from his battle with Tongariro for the love of the beautiful Pihanga on the shores of Lake Taupo. Set in the deep confines of these gorges, the Whanganui was a rich source of fish and vegetable foods for the early Maori, who some claim lived beside the river more than 800 years ago.

Early European settlers too used the river as a pathway to the interior with river steamers bringing tourists up to Pipiriki from the 1880s to the 1950s. From 1903 these steamers traded up from Whanganui as far as Taumarunui, the new town on the North Island Main Trunk Railway. Erosion, shallowing the river, gradually put a stop to this.

Visitors today favour kayaks, many entering the waters at Taumarunui for a five-day voyage downstream to Pipiriki. In this unroaded wilderness the river runs through a shaded succession of broad reaches interrupted by more than 200 rapids, each falling up to a metre. A narrow road from Raetihi meets the river at Pipiriki, then winds downstream above the river through a string of settlements renamed by missionaries, including Koriniti (Corinth), Ranana (London), Hiruharama (Jerusalem), and Atene (Athens).

Whanganui National Park of 74,000 hectares was established in 1986 to protect the surroundings of the river, and as a consequence the health of the great waterway itself. The actual riverbed and its waters are not part of the park, belonging instead to local Maori.

◀ OPPOSITE: *The Maori village of Hiruharama (Jerusalem) is built about a famous Catholic mission. The Whanganui here flows through areas of mixed forest and farmland.*

▲ *ABOVE: The main road from Raetihi reaches the Whanganui at Pipiriki. This is the downstream end of a five-day kayak journey from Taumarunui.*

Where pioneer farmers had sought to clear-fell or burn the forest, right up the edge of the gorges, now the riversides were to be specially protected, in part to halt erosion. There is plenty of evidence of the dangers of this, and the harsh conditions, particularly upstream, led to farmers failing and even walking off their land. The Bridge to Nowhere, built in 1936 and then abandoned, is seen now only from the water or by a rugged trampers' track — an isolated symbol of the aspirations and consequent defeat of pioneer farmers on the upper reaches of the river.

The forests protected by the national park are a mixture of giant podocarps and broad-leaved trees, with beech growing on the colder heights of the inland hills. The forests downstream from Pipiriki are regarded as some of the finest surviving lowland forests in New Zealand. Native birdlife is widespread, and a substantial population of brown kiwi is found even in the areas once cleared for farming but allowed to revert since the 1930s.

There is a point well downstream where the road rises and affords a view back over the now sinuous river. On a clear day, there is Ruapehu on the horizon, in the mountain cluster of Tongariro National Park. For the final 30 kilometres downstream, the river alters with the rise and fall of the tidal flow and ebb.

The coastal districts around Whanganui are farmland, but include a significant feature east of Kai Iwi where Forest and Bird has secured around 100 hectares of the original forest at Bushy Park. Ringed with a pest-excluder fence, the forest is managed as a bird sanctuary. Its burgeoning bird numbers include an introduced population of the endangered North Island saddleback, until recent years confined to a few pest-free islands, and North Island bush robin. Kiwi raised in captivity are also released here to give them a chance to grow safely into mature birds capable of defending themselves when released in the wild. The forest is dominated by rimu and matai, and includes what is claimed to be New Zealand's largest rata. Ratanui is 12 metres in girth and 43 metres tall.

Inland Whanganui is rugged country, much of it heavily eroded, where the frequent rivers have cut deep down through a former plateau of mudstones raised from the seabed. In the 1990s, it was proposed to extend Whanganui National Park over dense forests further north, east and south of the river. Though the land met the criteria for national park status, it was decided to defer any change until various Maori claims had been resolved. Meanwhile this land is protected in Crown reserves, with access at 11 road ends, and via the spectacular 'Forgotten World' road through the northern block, from Stratford in Taranaki via Whangamomona to Taumarunui on SH43.

▶ TOP RIGHT: *The giant northern rata tree, Ratanui, in the Forest and Bird reserve at Bushy Park. The reserve is in the Kai Iwi area northeast of Whanganui city.*

▶ RIGHT: *The vast inland forest areas east of Whanganui and Taranaki have been badly damaged in places by erosion after bush clearances.*

WELLINGTON

WELLINGTON

Wellington's wilderness is secured only in patches. The countryside from the Manawatu Plains to the capital is almost totally modified. Only the stern line of peaks inland serves as a reminder of what was once the wilderness.

The mountain backbone of the southern North Island runs south from the Manawatu Gorge to Wellington, by way of the Tararua, Ruahine and Rimutaka ranges. Individual peaks rise above 1200 metres, separating Wellington's west coast from southern Hawke's Bay and the Wairarapa. They are rugged and formidable, a challenging wilderness for the tramper, but the journey down the west coast by road runs largely through farmlands and finally the coast of Cook Strait. The few accessible 'wild patches' along this coast can be found by turning off the main road, particularly along the river estuaries.

The mouth of the Manawatu River, for example, is recognised under the Ramsar Agreement as a 'wetland of international importance'. Access via Foxton and Foxton Beach leads to saltmarsh and mudflats with a birdlist of 93 species. These include native waterbirds and wading birds, but also foreign migrants such as the eastern bar-tailed godwit.

The various beaches going south are of grey sand, their sandhills often rolling inland and converted to farmlands. The beaches sometimes carry the fractured frames of large trees, washed downstream from the interior. The poisonous but shy katipo spider may be found sheltering under flotsam in such places. Wading birds frequent the little estuaries and boggy patches, notably about the Waikanae river mouth which is a scientific reserve.

Waikanae faces Kapiti Island, arguably Wellington's wildlife showplace, about 5 kilometres off Paraparaumu Beach. It is open to the public by permit from the Department of Conservation, but daily numbers are limited and charter boats provide a restricted service.

▶ *OPPOSITE, TOP: Broad sandflats and riverbanks attract many wading birds, including migrants, to the estuary of the Manawatu River at Foxton. The area is a wetland of international importance.*

▶ *OPPOSITE, BOTTOM: Kapiti Island is 10 kilometres long but only 2 wide. At 1965 hectares, it is forested in regrowth except for a cleared Maori reserve over a flat area at the northern tip. The island rises in a long ridge to 521 metres at its peak, Tuteremoana.*

◀ *PAGES 158–159: The wild Wellington west coast is swept by frequent storms but it attracts fur seals (a colony at Red Rocks) and coastal native plants and lizards.*

Kapiti has been a reserve since the nineteenth century but pests including goats and deer ate it down to its roots over many years. The original podocarp forest has been replaced with kohekohe, tawa and kanuka. This regrowth forest provides a pest-free habitat for several rare birds put there so the public can observe them.

Kaka, the forest parrot, bounce about in the trees. More than 1000 little spotted kiwi have a safer home here than on the mainland where they are now thought to be extinct; birds from these survivors have also been transferred to some other offshore islands to establish additional populations.

Other rare or endangered birds introduced for safe-keeping include the takahe or notornis, North Island kokako, shore plover from the Chatham Islands, stitchbird, saddleback and brown teal. Other native bush birds include the red-crowned parakeet, the whitehead and North Island robin. Royal spoonbills nest here and frequent the adjacent mainland estuaries.

A marine reserve links Kapiti Island with the mainland at the Waikanae river mouth, and there is a further quadrant of marine reserve off the western side of the island. Clear water and varied habitats, particularly for colourful sponges, draw divers to these waters.

Further south off Plimmerton is Mana Island Scientific Reserve, also accessible by charter boat. It lies 2.5 kilometres offshore, an apparently flat island, but surrounded by steep cliffs. Once cleared as a grazing farm, the island is subject to a largely volunteer-based restoration

▲ TOP: *Relics of the shore whalers who based themselves about Kapit can still be traced in the coastal scrub. Stone walls mark the site of an old building.*

▲ ABOVE: *This whaling pot was used for boiling oil from the whale flesh.*

programme. Despite human occupation dating back to the fourteenth century, introduced mammals never got a hold here, except for vast numbers of mice. They were eradicated in 1990 as the Department of Conservation began making a refuge for threatened species such as Cook Strait giant weta, various skinks and geckos, the takahe and North Island robin. As the replanting matures more regional rarities are reintroduced, including wetland plants and animals in a purpose-built swamp.

On shore again the Porirua Harbour backs up beneath surrounding suburbs to the Pauatahanui Wildlife Reserve at its head. Here Forest and Bird and other volunteers have protected and planted marshlands and salt flats as habitat for breeding native fish and for wetland and migratory birds.

Heading down SH1 to Wellington there is little but spreading suburbia. Some flax swamps set in low valleys by the road include a privately covenanted reserve of harakeke flax or *Phormium tenax*.

The wild surprises of Wellington include two unusual reserves close inside the city, featuring native birds and plants, and an island in the harbour.

▼ BELOW: *Foxton Beach near the mouth of the Manawatu River. Recreational vehicles use the dunes and several beaches of the Wellington coast as roads. Here, as elsewhere, there are concerns over disturbing birds which roost or nest just above the tideline and for the health of shellfish beds.*

▲ *ABOVE: A former town water supply, the Karori Sanctuary focuses around a lake. Native trees are re-establishing but replanting programmes will enhance the habitat.*

The Karori Sanctuary, 'Zealandia', is within 10 minutes of Parliament but has wild populations of tuatara and little spotted kiwi, stitchbird and North Island saddleback. This unusual combination, within earshot of residents of suburban Karori, has been achieved by driving a pest-excluding fence around an old water reserve. While replanting with native trees is still underway the water reservoir, with its exotic pine trees, looks little like a native forest landscape, but the idea is working.

The pest-free fence excludes all the mammalian pests of New Zealand except mice (which are enemies of lizards and insects such as the weta). The fence runs 8.5 kilometres to enclose some 225 hectares of the valley. The footings include buried sections of fine-gauge netting either side of the fence to discourage dogs and other burrowing animals from finding their way underneath.

The reserve is now a safe place for releasing rare and endangered species. The only limitation is having enough suitable food and shelter for these introductions. The sanctuary's vision is a natural native forest evolving within 500 years: as close as possible to the way it was 'the day before humans arrived'.

The Otari-Wilton Bush reserve began with the vision of pioneer botanist Thomas Cockayne, who in 1926 established the gardens to contain specimens of every native plant and tree from the mainland and offshore. Labelled collections display the plants in family groups or in typical habitats from alpine to wetland and coastal. The gardens now shelter some 1200 species, hybrids and cultivars. The area adjoins a block of native forest under protection since 1860 and containing trees 400–500 years old.

Two islands in Wellington Harbour bear Maori names, following traditions of the Polynesian navigator Kupe exploring these coasts. Matiu/Somes Island, a scientific and historic reserve of 25 hectares, and Makaro/Ward Island are 'hilltops' in the drowned harbour, named after Kupe's daughters. Since the 1980s, Matiu/Somes has been restored for wildlife (and to recognise its successive role as Maori settlement, animal and human quarantine, wartime internment camp and defensive area). It is accessible by ferry from Wellington. The wild features of the island include restored coastal native plantings, pest-free habitat for lizards, and seabirds. Red-crowned parakeets, weta and tuatara are among releases of species from elsewhere.

Looking across Wellington's broad harbour from the city offers a longer view of the Rimutaka Range as it become the Orongorongo mountains and slide into the sea at Pencarrow Head. There is ready evidence of geological change in the uplifted platforms of the shingle coasts outside the harbour. The last spectacular movement in 1855 lifted the site of Wellington 8 metres, allowing the reclamation of several blocks of harbourside land. Ranges across the harbour also rose by 6 metres, creating a new shoreline there too.

A glance up the western edge of the Hutt Valley, with its shorn-off side ridges and cliffs, emphasises the frequency of movement along the Wellington Fault.

▲ *TOP: The curious kaka, a bush parrot, is common on Kapiti Island. Small flocks frequent the area near the boat landing.*

▲ *ABOVE: The pest-excluder fence which surrounds the urban bird sanctuary in Karori, Wellington. The bottom of the fence is buried to deter burrowing animals and the capping stops climbing pests. This technique is now being used on a number of projects to create mainland bird and lizard sanctuaries elsewhere.*

COOK STRAIT

THE FISH OF MAUI

The dangerous waters of Raukawa were crossed by Maori in wooden canoes as they traded greenstone from southern tribes, or on expeditions of conquest.

The North Island is regarded in Maori tradition as Te Ika a Maui, the fish of Maui. A map reveals the island has the shape of a skate with its mouth in Wellington Harbour, its eye in Lake Wairarapa and its fins protruding at Taranaki and East Cape. The tail of the fish is the long, thin land of Muriwhenua in the Far North.

The North Island was formed after the demi-god Maui sneaked aboard his brothers' boat with a fish hook made from the jawbone of his dead grandmother and baited with his own blood. The outline of the magic hook can still be seen in the cliffs jutting into Hawke Bay at Cape Kidnappers.

When Maui caught the North Island he wanted his giant fish blessed by a priest but his brothers disagreed. While Maui sought help, his brothers hacked into the floating fish, carving it into mountains and ravines. When Maui returned with a priest, the flesh of the giant catch had become the mountains and valleys of a rugged new island.

The South Island is regarded by some Maori as the canoe of Maui, with Stewart Island as its anchor stone. Southern Maori have a different story about their land's origins, however (see page 264).

Crossing Cook Strait (Raukawa in Maori) by car ferry affords a distant look at the adjacent land masses of the North and South islands. The open sea distance is only about 40 kilometres, with the rest of the voyage in the sheltered waters of the Marlborough Sounds.

Leaving Wellington Harbour the bleakness of this North Island coast is notable. The 5-metre uplift of the 1855 earthquake has created shingle beaches round the harbour, now used by local roads and rail. Outside the heads, lifted shorelines show how this coast is rising. (Turikirae Heads on the east coast of Wellington has risen 30 metres in the past 9000 years. The major uplifts are recorded in a rising series of old beaches.)

In the South Island the Kaikoura mountain ranges run for 100 kilometres south-ward. The largest mountain is Tapuae-o-uenuku at 2885 metres in the Inland Kaikoura Range. The Seaward Kaikoura Range includes Manakau at 2610 metres. On a clear day both ranges are visible from Wellington, 150 kilometres away.

The voyage across Cook Strait can offer the nature-lover the opportunity to watch for seabirds. Common near the travelling ships are black-backed gull, giant petrel and cape pigeon. Crossing the Strait, it can be possible to see a range of petrel and shearwaters, terns,

even Arctic skua, skimming the seas.

Fur-seal colonies on both the coasts of Cook Strait mean these animals may be seen during the voyage, but more likely are the dolphins and porpoises which populate these waters. The rare Hector's dolphin, bottle-nosed and dusky dolphins frequent these waters, along with passing orca, pilot and humpback whales.

During the ice ages, when sea levels were lower, the North and South islands were joined together from around Nelson to the Taranaki Bight. Across this land-bridge creatures such as the flightless moa and notornis could walk from North Island to South Island.

Since the rise of sea levels, with the last melting of the ice ages 10,000–12,000 years ago, populations of some birds have developed into separate subspecies on their 'new' islands. The tomtit and the kokako are examples of birds which have changed their appearance since the islands were separated by Cook Strait.

The last leg of the ferry voyage across Cook Strait is by way of the Marlborough Sounds. In contrast to the open waters of Raukawa, the Sounds appear as a maze of islands and hills, headlands and narrow waterways.

▲ TOP: *Leaving Wellington Harbour, Pencarrow Head is marked by two lights.*

▲ ABOVE: *Bird species sometimes developed in separate forms in the North and South Islands. The North Island kokako (front) has blue wattles while the extinct South Island subspecies had orange ones.*
Engraving by J.G. Keulemans from Walter Buller's *A History of the Birds of New Zealand.*

MARLBOROUGH

MARLBOROUGH SOUNDS

Motorists enter the South Island by a sea road, taking the vehicular ferry service from Wellington to Picton, through the Marlborough Sounds. Ships enter the Sounds in the northeast of the South Island, at Tory Channel, where the ruins of a whaling station abandoned in the 1960s huddle in a little bay just inside the East Head. The ferry then joins Queen Charlotte Sound on its voyage inland to Picton.

▲ *ABOVE: D'Urville Island lies just 500 metres off the northern Sounds. Tide races make the voyage through French Pass a difficult one with a navigable width of only 110 metres.*

◀ *PAGES 168–169: Parallel but separate waterways and twisting roads in the outer Sounds.*

The Marlborough Sounds offer a geographically intricate world comprising long islands and narrow waterways born from ancient geological movements, and rising sea levels since the last ice age. This is a drowned landscape. Maori saw the outline of shining water and islands as the pattern of light seen through the open carvings of a canoe sternpost: the remains of the foundered canoe of the gods which sank on its side to form the Southern Alps.

While much of the original wilderness is compromised by land clearance and pine plantations, in scenic terms the experience of sailing up to Picton through the narrow seaways is dramatic.

Keep the binoculars handy for the sweeping flocks of seabirds which fish these waterways. By the entrance to the Sounds look for king shag among the more familiar species. Totalling around 500 birds, the king shag population is peculiar to the outer islands and reefs of the Marlborough Sounds.

The Marlborough Sounds are the flooded northeast continuation of the Richmond and Bryant Ranges which lie between Nelson and Marlborough. Here they disappear into the sea. Long arms of the sea run parallel with each other,

▲ *ABOVE: South Island saddleback.*

ranging to the northeast. Flooded valleys between them may be blocked by islands, a low isthmus, or dangerous reefs.

While narrow, winding roads run out to some of these extremities, the Marlborough Sounds are best explored from the sea. Too often the gravel roads are both demanding and boring as they run along ridges of cleared farmland and introduced pines. The natural areas are serviced by charter trips and tours from both Picton and Havelock.

Lieutenant James Cook on the ship *Endeavour* claimed the South Island of New Zealand for Britain by raising a flag on tiny Motuara, an island in the mouth of Queen Charlotte Sound. (His masters didn't want his new possession, however.) Motuara today is a wildlife reserve visited by tour boats.

At nearby Ship Cove, Cook careened the *Endeavour* while the expedition botanist described the plants and the people

BIRD ISLAND

Motuora, off Ship Cove, is now a wildlife refuge visited by tour boats. The former farmland has reverted to coastal forest. Introduced pests have been removed and native birds re-established.

Rarities include the South Island saddle-back/tieke and bush robin/toutouwai. The dawn chorus of birds, described here by Joseph Banks in 1770, is being restored with burgeoning bird populations including bell-bird/korimako, tui and other native forest birds. By the wharf, and in artificial nest boxes along the track, little blue penguins nest.

Animal introductions to the island include Maud Island frog and Marlborough green gecko.

▲ *ABOVE: The shoreline of Motuara, the island where Cook claimed the South Island for Britain. It is now a predator-free wildlife refuge.*

SPOILT FOR CHOICE

The Wairau Valley route (SH63) climbs gradually to St Arnaud at 600 metres, and the headquarters of the Nelson Lakes National Park. This is also the beginning of the Buller region, with SH63/SH6 continuing to Murchison and Westland. The Lewis Pass route to Canterbury also follows SH6 but turns off southward shortly beyond Murchison onto SH65.

Alternatively, head north for Nelson via SH6 at Kawatiri or take the back road via Tophouse and the Golden Downs forestry.

State Highway 1 from Picton crosses the Wairau Valley at Blenheim and heads directly south to Christchurch via the Kaikoura coast.

who lived there. The rare king shag may be seen on the low cliffs nearby.

Goats and sheep liberated by Cook's expeditions in the early 1770s heavily damaged the nature of Arapawa Island (on the northern shore of the ferry entrance to the Marlborough Sounds). When they were culled some 200 years later, people interested in rare breeds kept a sample flock of what they believed would be survivors of the extinct Old English milk goat.

Farther out, on the Cook Strait coasts of the Sounds, isolated island groups and rocks have been declared absolute sanctuaries for wildlife. Stephens Island (Takapourewa), for example, has a huge population of more than 30,000 tuatara. These creatures are the only animal survivors of the age of dinosaurs. Unchecked, the tuatara are blamed for the extinction of a number of native insects on the island as their population approached 1500 to 2000 per hectare; in places that density is now 3000 tuatara to the hectare. Many share their burrows with fairy prion. The native Hamilton's

frog survives there too. Once Stephens Island had its own species of wren, discovered only when the first lighthouse keeper was presented by his cat with the bodies of the last survivors.

The North Brothers, one of a group of islets glimpsed from the ferry just before it enters Tory Channel, has its own subspecies of tuatara. A seamark for early navigators entering the Sounds, the Brothers are regarded as tapu by Maori, who in the past put out the eyes of lowly crew members who looked upon them.

Maud Island (Te Hoiere) has been used as a refuge in the restoration of rare and endangered wildlife since 1974. The first introductions were of notornis or takahe, an ancient rail believed extinct till it was rediscovered in the Murchison Mountains of Fiordland in 1948.

For 20 years, various kakapo — the endangered, nocturnal ground parrot — were also held on Maud Island; they were about to be transferred when they began to breed and now there are several juveniles in a national population of around 125. Maud Island also has its own species of

▲ *ABOVE: The waters of Port Underwood, southernmost of the Sounds. Whaling from shore stations was established here in the mid 1820s.*

▼ *BELOW: Tuatara basking at the mouth of its burrow. It is vulnerable to rats and is largely restricted to a few pest-free islands such as Stephens Island. This specimen was photographed at Lady Alice Island, Northland.*

native frog, the pakeka, which has been managed to an estimated population of 19,000 and introduced to tiny Motuara nearby. Cook Strait giant weta have been introduced, along with giant snails, a rare hebe and a click beetle.

D'Urville Island (Rangitoto Ke Te Tonga), the largest of the Marlborough islands, sits just 500 metres off the north coast. Here there is a tide race where Cook Strait currents sweep through to Tasman Bay at up to 7 knots. Its name, French Pass, recalls the day in 1827 when the French navigator Dumont d'Urville sailed his ship through the narrow gap, which has a navigable width of 110 metres, and hit the edges of a reef twice before bouncing through. Despite this, the French Pass route was later used by steam ferry services between Wellington and Nelson. From 1888 till 1912 a Risso's dolphin nicknamed Pelorus Jack became famous for accompanying ships passing through.

A road route from Picton winds along the upper shores of Queen Charlotte Sound and passes over a low saddle to Havelock, which is sited on a further network of drowned valleys. Again, while there are winding roads along some of the peninsulas, it is much more enjoyable to take a tour by sea.

Havelock is near the mouth of the Pelorus River, which rises in the Mt Richmond Forest Park on the Rai Valley/Whangamoa route to Nelson. At Pelorus Bridge, walking tracks wind through fine reserves of beech trees which crowd down to the rock-sided river gorge. This is a good place to see native bush birds, including weka.

The broad Wairau Valley constitutes the bulk of Marlborough's flat country. After rising between two ranges of the Southern Alps, the Wairau River turns east and races for 100 kilometres to enter the sea south of the Marlborough Sounds. Its shingle riverbed follows a faultline ruled along the foot of the Richmond Ranges, which divide Marlborough from Nelson. Once tussock grassland, the dry climate and stony river soils of the Wairau Valley now produce fine wines, sauvignon blanc varietals in particular.

The Richmond Ranges, parallel to the river, have been drifting along the faultline of the Southern Alps for millions of years. A curiosity in the upper Wairau valleys is Red Hill (1791 metres), consisting of the same mineral-rich rocks which appear on the opposite side of the fault in the Red Hills of South Westland. It is argued these mountains were originally one, and that the shearing movement along the Alpine Fault has now moved the two sides 480 kilometres apart. The soils of these parts of the 'ultramafic' or mineral belt are laden with iron, manganese, nickel and cobalt, forced up from the mantle of the earth by some tectonic cataclysm. Both Red Hill areas have similar vegetation, specially adapted to tolerate the high-mineral content of ultramafic rocks.

The full Wairau Valley route leads directly to Nelson Lakes National Park and inland routes to the West Coast, Canterbury, and Nelson to the north.

ALTERNATIVE ROUTE

Havelock and Pelorus Bridge can also be reached from Blenheim by a longer but easier route (SH6 to Nelson), travelling first through vineyards up the Wairau Valley and bypassing the upper reaches of Queen Charlotte Sound.

▲ TOP: Natural history boat tours of Queen Charlotte Sound pass the nesting place of king shag (centre and left), a species peculiar to the outer Sounds.

▲ ABOVE: The navigator James Cook repaired his ship Endeavour in the Marlborough Sounds in 1770. The site, Ship Cove in Queen Charlotte Sound, is marked by the Cook Memorial.

▲ ABOVE: An orchard of old karaka trees dating from Maori settlement backs the beach at Ship Cove.

NELSON

N E L S O N   L A K E S
N A T I O N A L   P A R K

The high-country lakes, Rotoiti and Rotoroa, fill the beds of ancient glaciers which once ground down the northern tangle of the Southern Alps. Sparkling Rotoiti lies between the beech-clad walls of the St Arnaud and Travers ranges. Rotoroa, the long lake, is gloomier, surrounded by wetland forest at its outlet, and drawing its waters from farther inland. The two lakes and the looming blue peaks above them have been a national park since 1956. Some 102,000 hectares of mountain wilderness, inaccessible except on foot, are protected by the park. The lakes, however, are easy to approach by road.

Rotoiti is the source of the mighty Buller River which flows to the West Coast. The Rotoroa catchment feeds the racing whitewater of the Gowan River, another Buller tributary. There are memorable forest walks about both lakes and launch access to the headwaters of both. In these remote upper valleys, crystal-clear rivers and tarns sparkle through a fretwork of beech branches, beneath towering mountains.

Smaller Rotoiti is the easiest to explore, with several tracks, including a day walk around its shores and another clambering through the natural succession of beech forests to the alpine tops of the St Arnaud Range at 1600–1800 metres. The lake itself lies at 600 metres above sea level and covers around 1000 hectares.

Rotoiti is a popular place for holiday-makers, for water sports, angling, and skiing on bald Mt Robert in winter.

Close to the township of St Arnaud, the Department of Conservation has been

▲ *ABOVE: Lake Rotoiti viewed from the walking track above the bushline of the St Arnaud Range. The infant Buller River rises here and passes through the high grass plain beyond.*

◀ *OPPOSITE: The crest of the St Arnaud Range lies above the snowline, with tussocks and mountain flowers in summer. Below is the Wairau River heading toward Marlborough.*

◀ *PAGES 176–177: Marahau at the southern entry to Abel Tasman National Park, Nelson.*

▲ ABOVE: *Red and silver beech forest alongside Rotoiti is in a special wildlife management area.*

experimenting with a 'mainland island' to help recover the ecology of the beech forests. Intensive pest management is directed at controlling runaway populations of introduced European wasps, and mammals such as stoats, possums and deer.

The wasps steal the honeydew produced by a scale insect which lives on the bark of the beech trees, coating the bark in what looks like soot. The wasps, accidentally introduced in the 1950s, feed on the drops of honeydew produced by the scale insects, to the detriment of native insects (which otherwise provide bird food) and honey-eating birds. Early on, conservation operators destroyed 2300 wasp nests (1.7 million wasps) to reduce their population over a mere 827 hectares. That achieved a 90 percent 'knockdown' of the wasps but the process

needs to be repeated every few years.

At the same time, traps and baits were laid to control populations of introduced rats, possums and stoats. The kaka, a forest-dwelling parrot, smaller parakeets and yellowhead/mohua are particularly vulnerable to these introduced pests because they are hole-nesting birds easily caught and killed at the nest. As a result of the early pest control kaka numbers rose markedly. The Kerr Bay area beside St Arnaud is the place to hear native birds such as tui, bellbird and kaka calling in the daylight, and to see rifleman, pied tit and bush robin feeding fearlessly along the track.

During the past 10 years, the pest-controlled area of this mainland island has been extended to 5000 hectares, a huge achievement in these rugged forest valleys, but such pest management covers only a tiny fraction of the extensive beech forests that clothe the South Island high country, and where similar problems exist.

Rotoroa — the long lake — is narrower than Rotoiti, but runs 15 kilometres up to its headwaters. The valleys of the Sabine and D'Urville rivers feed Rotoroa with the snow-melt and run-off from a vast isolated region at the end of the Southern Alps toward the Spenser Mountains. The lake is twice the size of Rotoiti, at 2100 hectares, and lies at an altitude of 451 metres. Beyond the mixed rainforest at its outlet, where giant rata and kahikatea rise above raupo wetlands, the lake is bounded by sheer mountains, clad from shore to snowline in dense beech forest.

▲ *TOP: The headwaters of Lake Rotoroa rise in the isolated gorges of the Southern Alps.*

▶ *RIGHT: Dense beech forests towering above the headwaters of Rotoroa. The forest succession rises from red beech through extensive silver beech forests. Nearer the snowline small and hardy black or mountain beech grow.*

BULLER RIVER

The Buller River sweeps over the lip of Rotoiti and carries the run-off from its mountainous forest catchment swiftly to the sea. Regarded as New Zealand's fifth-largest river, it can quickly swell in flood to carry a larger volume of water than any other river in the country.

From Rotoiti, the Buller makes a 170 kilometre journey to its river mouth at Westport on the Tasman coast. The river's Maori name, Kawatiri, has been fittingly translated as 'deep and swift'. Nearly half of its course runs through deep gorges between rocky cliffs overhung by forested hillsides.

Initially the Buller runs a rapid race across tussock shrublands, gathering the force of the Hope River coming from the north at Kawatiri (at a T-junction with SH6 running north to Nelson and south to Murchison). At Gowanbridge the rushing whitewater of the tumbling Gowan adds the watershed of another lake, Rotoroa.

The now deep and swirling waters of the Buller flow at the foot of steep forested gorges overhung with patches of podocarp forest and beech trees down to Murchison and the Four Rivers Plain. Here it is joined by further rivers born in the Spenser Mountains to the south, and the remote southern edges of Kahurangi National Park which stand to the north above the alluvial plains. Gold was mined here until the 1940s, leaving the tell-tale 'tailings' of re-sorted river stones beneath the blackberry and bracken.

The hillsides about Murchison are broken and twisted following the impact of a tremendous earthquake (7.8 on the Richter scale) in 1929. The earthquake triggered huge landslides, tumbling house-sized blocks of rock down the steep gullies, and redirecting the courses of rivers such as the Matukituki and Maruia to create new lakes and waterfalls. Despite the district's sparse population, 17 people died.

The Buller River is now cutting into the river terraces at the northern edge of Murchison, having in early days wiped out a pioneer settlement on the river flats below.

The Upper Buller Gorge carves through the Brunner and Lyell ranges before reaching open country again around Inangahua Junction. The Murchison earthquake fractured the road through the Upper Gorge, uplifting one section 4.5 metres. Living landslips in the forest reflect rockfalls from more recent quakes.

A reminder of the geological instability of the area occurs at Inangahua, another area of open country with a major river joining the Buller. In 1968, a magnitude seven earthquake severely damaged parts of the town, triggering landslides along the Buller, and taking three lives.

In 1847, Nelson explorer Thomas Brunner was the first European to venture into this inhospitable landscape. It took him and his four Maori companions three months to find their way downstream, a journey that now takes a couple of hours by car. The Upper Gorge from Murchison to Inangahua took them six weeks to negotiate, living for days largely on fern root. They then encountered the Lower Buller Gorge, below Inangahua, and took six further weeks to negotiate the river walls of the Paparoa Range. Here they were so short of food they finally ate Brunner's dog to survive.

It is still easily possible to appreciate the effort involved in that journey, looking at the swirling river confined within canyon walls and overrunning giant granite rocks. The road still follows the narrow way carved into the side of Hawks Crag to negotiate a bend above the river. Brunner complained of negotiating such precipices high above the water, and the lack of food to be found in the black beech forests hanging almost vertically above.

The last 14 kilometres of the Buller runs through comparatively open country. This tidal stretch of the river is the haunt of migratory whitebait, or inanga, the fingerlings of which are netted in spring as a delicacy. On the north shore of the Buller river mouth an extensive lagoon and wetland protects native waterbirds. To the south, there is a seal colony at Cape Foulwind, where the woodhen, weka, is conspicuous along the tracks.

(See Westland chapter for the coastal journey and Paparoa National Park.)

▲ TOP: *The Buller winds through its deep upper gorge above Lyell.*

▲ ABOVE: *Wrought-iron grave markers are all that survives of Lyell, once a gold-mining town on the Buller.*

KAHURANGI &
NORTHWEST NELSON

The northwest of Nelson is a wilderness of rugged mountains and forest land but its borders are fascinating places to explore. Two national parks and further coastal reserves protect its nature.

Most of the land between Farewell Spit, at the top of the South Island, and the Buller River, 125 kilometres to the south, is protected in the public conservation estate.

Native forests rise from mixed rainforest to extensive beech forests and a number of spectacular tussock plateaux accessed only by demanding tramping tracks. In places, the rugged landscape is shaped by uplifted karst landscapes of marble and limestone. Elsewhere, sedimentary rocks are twisted and flooded by earthquakes, or disturbed by volcanic intrusions and the effects of glaciation.

Kahurangi National Park is New Zealand's second-largest national park at more than 500,000 hectares. Yet, in all of Nelson, Golden Bay, Buller and Westland, road access to the park occurs at only 12 points around the boundaries. Tramping track entries generally lie at the end of long, winding and shingle roads. The Flora Saddle, for example, is accessed by a steep road inland from Motueka, and is the starting point for fine walks up to the

high point of Mt Arthur (1795 metres), or a two-day, cross-country walk to the head of Lake Cobb on the Golden Bay side of Takaka Hill.

Mt Arthur is a massif of marble and its

▲ *ABOVE: The Cobb River at the road end from Upper Takaka.*

◀ *OPPOSITE: Water shaped these fluted marble landforms atop Takaka Hill. The marble mountains of Kahurangi National Park are distinguished by raw outcrops of marble, sinkholes and giant cave systems.*

flanks bear obvious signs of sinkholes. Among the cave systems inside the mountain, Nettlebed has been probed to a depth of 889 metres with more than 24 kilometres of passages mapped; the Ellis Basin system has more than 28 kilometres. (Further south, above the Buller River, the Bulmer Chasm of Mt Owen (1875 metres) is the longest cave system in New Zealand with 50 kilometres of passageways and a depth of 749 metres.)

North of Nelson, SH60 winds over Takaka Hill from Riwaka to Golden Bay, cresting at nearly 800 metres. In this land of moving mists, fluted marble outcrops are indicative of the water-shaped karst landscapes beneath.

A side road to Canaan Downs runs 11 kilometres along the crest of the mountain range through forests and tussock marked with marble outcrops. This road in turn leads by a short walk to the rim of Harwood's Hole. Here water has worn a sinkhole 357 metres down into Takaka Hill, and another of the cave systems that honeycomb the mountain.

On the northern side of Takaka Hill — popularly called the Marble Mountain — is Golden Bay, with tortuous access to Lake Cobb (with its trilobite fossils, New Zealand's oldest), and to the valley of the Aorere River (starting point of the Heaphy Track to the West Coast).

There is road access at Pakawau, beyond Collingwood, to the west coast

▶ RIGHT: *Dawn on a tussock plateau above the snowline in Kahurangi National Park, between the Flora Saddle road and Lake Cobb.*

▲ *ABOVE: Sinkholes in the side of Mt Arthur are clues to the extensive cavern systems below.*

harbour known as Whanganui Inlet. This is remote country with scattered settlement. The harbour is refuge to wetland and wading birds. Mangarakau Swamp is a reserve for them.

Farthest north on SH60, the public road ends at Puponga Farm Park, a 470-hectare stretch of rolling, open country with patches of wetland and coastal forest. Stimulating walks across country include tracks to the rocks and crashing surf of the open Tasman Sea at Wharariki Beach and Fossil Point. The swamps are home to bitterns, marsh crake and fernbirds.

FAREWELL SPIT

To go beyond Puponga onto Farewell Spit, it is necessary to take a commercial eco-tour from Collingwood. Built up over 14,000 years, from glacial sands swept north along the West Coast, Farewell Spit is a notable haunt of migratory birds.

The Spit projects in a curve shaped like the beak of a kiwi, protecting Golden Bay from the assaults of the Tasman Sea. Its dunes and beaches reach out into the ocean for more than 25 kilometres. In places the Spit is up to a kilometre wide even when the tide is high. When the tide falls, its dunes protect extensive sandflats up to 10 kilometres broad inside Golden Bay. These low-tide mudflats provide more than 9000 hectares of feeding grounds for tens of thousands of birds. The Spit is recognised as a wetland of international significance under the Ramsar Convention. Besides the flocks of Arctic birds which summer there, Australasian gannets nest and breed on the Spit, almost at sea level.

▲ *TOP: The wild Tasman Sea attacks the western shore of Puponga Farm Park which runs, coast to coast, between Kahurangi National Park and Farewell Spit.*

▲ *ABOVE: Bones of the extinct moa are displayed on the floor of a small cavern on Takaka Hill. Speleologists have found the bones of many extinct species which have fallen through sinkholes from the surface of caves in karst country.*

▶ *RIGHT: Caves honeycomb much of the marble country. A short public cave walk near the summit of Takaka Hill explores the ground beneath the marble outcrops.*

ABEL TASMAN NATIONAL PARK

The township of Takaka provides the only road access into Abel Tasman National Park, New Zealand's smallest at 19,222 hectares. Abel Tasman is a much gentler place than Kahurangi and is best known for its superb coastline of golden sands and picturesque rock formations. The park runs round the coast from Golden Bay to Tasman Bay. While it is reasonably forested in beech species and some podocarps, much of it was felled in pioneering days, before the park was established, and is now in the process of regeneration. There are still some isolated private enclaves on the coast.

Abel Tasman National Park was established in 1942 to mark the tercentenary of the European discovery of New Zealand by Abel Janszoon Tasman of the Dutch East India Company. Tasman anchored off the Tata Islands but could not land. His expedition was driven off by local Maori, who killed some of his crew while they attempted to row between his two ships. Now the coast is best known as one of New Zealand's 'Great Walks', and for the sheltered canoeing and boating provided by its shallow waterways and offshore islets. Small whales and dolphins frequent this coast along with fur seals.

Road access is only possible to park headquarters at Totaranui by following the coast east from Takaka via Pohara. Takaka is a Maori name for the bracken fern, the roots of which were gathered and ground as a staple food by early Maori. The journey is winding and sometimes rough, and as there may be nowhere to camp in summer, booking beforehand is recommended. Abel Tasman National Park can also be entered by launch services operating from the southern border of the park out of Marahau and Kaiteriteri but there is no road access beyond this point. The Abel Tasman 'Great Walk' follows the coastline from Marahau to Totaranui (and someway beyond if desired). The route follows gentle beaches and estuaries with occasional low saddles between bays.

Booking with the Department of Conservation is necessary. This is a 'pay for' walk, much in demand with trampers going in either direction, though day walking is free. The Abel Tasman Track is 52 kilometres long and takes 3–5 days.

◀ OPPOSITE: *The sheltered waters and islets of Abel Tasman National Park attract many kayakers and boating enthusiasts, as well as people undertaking the five-day walk around the coast.*

▲ TOP: *Much of the 'Great Walk' is level, following beaches and skirting bays.*

▲ ABOVE: *Picturesque rock formations and golden sands set the relaxed atmosphere of the coastal walk.*

▲ *ABOVE: The succession of tides may affect the course of the journey.*

◀ *LEFT: The Pupu Springs lie off SH60 in the valley of the Waikoropupu River 8, kilometres northwest of Takaka. Among the largest freshwater springs in the world, they produce more than 2600 million litres a day. The water 'bubbles up', as one version of the Maori name suggests, from two main pools and from other springs fed by water brought underground from the limestone/marble mountains.*

KAIKOURA COAST

KAIKOURA COAST

The spectacular drive along the Kaikoura coast runs beside the ocean, dwarfed by the looming bulk of the Seaward Kaikoura Range. To begin, driving south through the bone-coloured hills of Marlborough, the road passes the extensive pink pans where the sun evaporates salt at Lake Grassmere. The sensational views of snow-capped mountains begin where the road runs down to the coast.

This is the edge of a rugged, mountainous tract of country. Some 500,000 hectares of mountains and high-country valleys extend inland to the Southern Alps, along the Lewis Pass and Nelson Lakes National Park.

From the coastal highway, the Seaward Kaikoura Range is the most conspicuous of these ranges, rising to 2600 metres. Running parallel to it, the Inland Kaikoura Range reaches beyond 2700 metres. The bulk of its highest peak, Tapuae-o-uenuku, at 2885 metres can often be seen from as far away as Wellington, standing above its hulking neighbours as a snow-clad prominence. Its close neighbour Mt Alarm is nearly as high at 2865 metres.

The inland high country, between and beyond the Kaikoura ranges, is a spectacular region of tussock grasslands, alpine shrubs and crumbling mountainsides. The

▼ BELOW: *Pilot whales are among the several species spotted from the whale-watching boats.*

succession of inland ranges parallel to the seacoast are divided by faultlines down which run the Awatere and Clarence rivers. The Awatere flows to the sea north of the Kaikoura coast, near Seddon, while the Clarence rounds the northern end of the Seaward Kaikoura Range and flows circuitously down a shingle delta to the sea about 35 kilometres north of Kaikoura.

This inland high country, valuable as it is as near wilderness, is basically inaccessible to the motorist. Roads indicated through Molesworth Station — at 180,000 hectares New Zealand's largest farm and now a high-country park — and another road through Rainbow Station even further inland, are restricted to four-wheel-drive vehicles. These routes are rarely opened because of weather and fire restrictions.

New Zealand's latest round of mountain-building — earthquakes are a frequent indication that the process is still going on — is known as the Kaikoura Orogeny after the upthrusting of these geologically young mountains. The uplift began about five million years ago and is presently believed to be about a metre every century. In places the greywacke mountains are so raw they are bare of soil and the unstable rocks collapse in shingle slides and rockfalls as the winter snows melt. The faultlines between the mountain ranges are also moving against each other, some argue by as much as 50 mm a year.

Sheltered mountain valleys along the foothills of the Seaward Kaikoura Range still contain substantial remnants of beech forest and mixed coastal forest, but most of the focus here is on the wild coast. North of the Clarence River, mountain streams bound out of rocky gullies onto

▲ *ABOVE: At Kaikoura the rugged shore consists of distorted layers of sharp rock, often twisted to the vertical. The Kaikoura Peninsula itself is capped with limestone. It was once an island, subsequently joined to the mainland by the outwash of rocks from the eroding mountains.*

◀ *PAGES 194–195: The healthy fur seal colonies of Kaikoura skirt the coast. Parking bays look straight down on them.*

▲ *ABOVE: Ocean seabirds are attracted to a bird-watching boat by offerings of supplementary food.*

WHALE WATCHING

The waters of the Kaikoura Canyon are the best place in New Zealand to watch whales and the seabirds which also feed there.

Sperm whales up to 20 metres long frequent these waters year round. Their spectacular flukes rise from the water as they tip over to dive up to 300 metres deep in the underwater canyon in search of fish. Every 50 minutes or so the whales rise again to 'blow' and take in air for their next dive.

Other whales pass through these productive waters on their migrations into the Pacific to breed. The migrants include blue whales, humpback whales, southern right and pilot whales. Orca, sometimes known as killer whales, also pass along this coast.

The conditions which attract the whales also attract dusky dolphins, which hunt in schools, sometimes of a hundred or more, feeding on fish. There is also a resident population of the world's rarest and smallest dolphin, Hector's dolphin, which is only 1.6 metres long.

steep shingle fans, sometimes damaging road and rail links when flash floods surge to the sea. The road runs beneath the mountains, overlooking dunes and long shingle beaches, until it reaches the mouths of the Clarence River. It then hugs a rocky coast where the sea surges through reefs barely softened by beds of trailing kelp.

The coastal town of Kaikoura has built its fortunes in recent decades from the natural deep-sea wonders just offshore. The town is a tourist centre for offshore boat trips to see ocean birds, whales and seals. Land trips penetrate the Seaward Kaikoura Range, while there are fascinating walks around the coast of the Kaikoura Peninsula where seals haul out and seabirds roost.

A whaling settlement in the nineteenth century, Kaikoura lies at a point where deep ocean water brings the whales close to shore. The underwater Kaikoura Canyon falls to 1000 metres below sea level, within a kilometre of the rocky shore. Upwellings of cold water from these depths bring masses of krill to the surface, attracting baleen whales. Rich shoals of fish and other marine creatures such as squid also feed on the krill, attracting in turn toothed whales and dolphins which feed on them.

Ocean birds too are attracted by the abundance of food. Various species of albatross, some still known locally as mollymawks, sweep low over the waters as do giant petrels and other petrel and shearwater relatives. Some 13 species of albatross, including the endangered wandering albatross, 14 different petrels and seven shearwater species have been recorded.

A curiosity of the region is the Hutton's shearwater, which is one of the few ocean birds still to nest on the mainland. Some 100,000 pairs make their breeding tunnels high up in the Seaward Kaikoura Range, among the snow tussocks and alpine vegetation between 1200 and 1800 metres. The migratory birds return to their ancestral breeding grounds from late August when there is often snow on the ground, and the young fledge in March–early April.

New Zealand fur seals are commonly seen in coastal waters. They roll and dive amongst the kelp beds and often come ashore to bask on the giant rocks below the road. There is a lively colony on reefs around the Kaikoura Peninsula, easily viewable from the peninsula walkway. A further breeding colony, where in summer a few adults supervise a kindergarten of young seals, can be readily watched from a parking area south of Kaikoura.

Colonies of red-billed gulls occupy

▲ TOP: *Fyffe House, Kaikoura, is a relic of the early whaling days. It sits on foundations made from the spinal bones of whales.*

▲ ABOVE: *A whale-bone gatepost is among other relics at the house.*

▲ *ABOVE: A New Zealand fur seal colony south of Kaikoura. Here young seals are supervised in a 'creche' by some of the females while most of the parents are at sea fishing.*

▶ *OPPOSITE: The Seaward Kaikoura Range looms over the Kaikoura coast, rising at its highest to Manakau at 2610 metres and Te Ao Whekere at 2596 metres. Whale rib-bones on the esplanade recall the town's origin as a coastal whaling station.*

rock stacks and islets just offshore. White-fronted terns also nest on ledges above the sea. Black and little shags are common.

Just south of Kaikoura, the Maori Leaping Caves are named for the feat of a warrior who jumped 30 metres over a cliff to escape an enemy. The caves are a limestone formation, in an old marine cliff-face, complete with stalactites and stalagmites. They contain fossil seal and penguin bones.

From Kaikoura south the road is soon thrust against the sea again by steep coastal hills. Passengers may watch for seals and seabirds but drivers need to concentrate on the road, which often hangs just above the rock reefs of the sea. In places the road even divides into south- and north-bound tunnels to negotiate the rugged headlands.

At Oaro the road turns inland, winding over the Hundalee hills, and into the gold and brown pastures of Canterbury. Pause in the signposted reserves to see small bush birds including bellbirds, tomtits and in some places, bush robins.

EATING CRAYFISH

Kaikoura is a shortened form of the original Maori placename, Te ahi kai koura a Tamatea Pokai Whenua. It recalls the occasion when the Maori explorer Tamatea Pokai Whenua lit fires here and cooked crayfish. The Kaikoura coast is still well known for this delicacy.

CANTERBURY

▲ ABOVE: *The high-country headwaters of a Canterbury river. Shingle washed out from the U-shaped valleys of ancient glaciers has filled the valley floor, flattening it. The streams of the river wander across the riverbed in ever-changing 'braids'. Rare and endangered birds nest in dynamic landscapes like this.*

◀ PAGES 202–203: *Lyttelton Harbour fills the craters of an extinct volcano, on Banks Peninsula, Canterbury.*

CANTERBURY

The vast Canterbury Plains, sloping imperceptibly down from the foothills of the Southern Alps, are no longer a wilderness. Agriculture has stripped the pioneer covering of giant tussock and dryland shrubs, turning all into productive fields, many lined with gorse hedges and shelter belts of introduced pine.

Yet before the tussock grasslands encountered by Europeans in the 1850s, this land too was forest, much of it totara. This ancient forest is believed to have burned in the fourteenth century during 'the fires of Tamatea', reputedly set by the early Maori explorer Tamatea Pokai Whenua to clear the land. Burnt stumps of this old forest may still be found in the foothills, buried in the remnants of old grasslands. Such tussocklands now stretch across the hills from North Canterbury into Central Otago.

The Canterbury Plains are built of the stones and gravels washed down from the Southern Alps, and dusted with the loess borne from the mountains by floods and the nor'west winds.

Huge rivers born in the snowfields and glaciers of the Southern Alps burst through mountain gorges and cross the plains directly to the sea. Crossing the plains they spill over broad shingle riverbeds a kilometre or more wide. The islands in these braided rivers are now often choked with European weeds, pests such as lupin, broom, gorse and willow. The impact of these changes has been to further diminish the wildlife habitat available for the migratory wading birds which breed there.

Despite the changes wrought by settlement, however, there are still two areas which attract visitors in search of wild New Zealand. The headwaters of the 'braided' rivers often flow through broad grassland basins among alpine 'foothills' which are themselves significant mountain ranges. There are also the extinct volcanoes of Banks Peninsula, on the seaward edge of the plains, which rise above Christchurch, enclosing long harbours and providing sheltered places for wildlife.

The spring-fed Avon and Heathcote rivers of Christchurch wander sinuously through the low-lying city, which was built on a flax swamp. The rivers meet in the Avon–Heathcote Estuary where thousands of migratory wading birds gather. Some 113 different kinds of shorebird have been recorded there. The Bromley oxidation ponds are a good place to see birds. In recent years the urban reaches of the Avon River have developed a flourishing population of the New Zealand scaup or black teal, more usually found in scattered populations focused on lakes.

BANKS

PENINSULA

The bulk of the drowned volcanoes of Lyttelton and Akaroa rise steeply above Christchurch at the sea-edge of the Canterbury Plains. To the explorer James Cook, observing from 10 miles offshore, this was Banks Island which he named after his botanist, Sir Joseph Banks.

Cook was not too far wrong in his guess. While the volcanoes rose from the sea millions of years before the formation of the Canterbury Plains, they have only been connected to the mainland in the last 15,000 years or so, with the passing of the last ice age.

Banks Peninsula has the classic shape of a large shield volcano with its craters and valleys drowned by the rising sea. The overall mass of about 1200 square kilometres is nibbled all round its circumference by steep and rugged valleys falling into rocky harbours. Lyttelton and Akaroa are by far the largest, both centres of volcanic eruptions millions of years ago, but now deeply eroded and filled by the sea. The highest peak, Mt Herbert (919 metres) at the centre of the peninsula, is the source of the youngest volcanoes.

The volcanoes of Banks Peninsula may have begun 90 million years ago but their form today began 15–20 million years ago around the head of Lyttelton Harbour. The giant Lyttelton volcano dates from

◀ *LEFT: Volcanic cliffs front the outer edge of Banks Peninsula. Local roads are steep and twisting, usually gravel. Some end in private farmland, not the beach.*

▲ TOP: *Akaroa Harbour is another drowned volcano, lying back to back with Lyttelton.*

▲ ABOVE: *Dykes of extruded lava project from the walls of the Port Hills above Christchurch. The hills are the northern edge of the Lyttelton volcano.*

about 12 million years ago and may have reached 1500 metres in height over some two million years before it eroded away. The drowned Akaroa volcano dates back some nine million years. Mt Herbert volcano, standing between the two giant harbours, erupted some 5.8 million years ago.

This rugged place has its own distinct climate, windswept and snow-capped in winter, with its peaks rising to around 500 metres on the Port Hills above Christchurch and several peaks to around 700–800 metres toward Akaroa. Fogs can enter the valleys from the sea, and often swirl around the peaks when these are not swept by strong winds. Tawny tussocks protect much of the wilderness landscape.

The Summit Road around the northern crater rim of Lyttelton reveals a rugged, volcanic landscape with old peaks, volcanic dykes and eroded cliffs steeply overhanging the long harbour. The vertiginous view is in complete contrast to the opposing view over the 60 kilometre width of the Canterbury Plains which run blandly inland to the foothills of the Southern Alps.

Highway 75 to Akaroa winds its way over Hilltop to reveal another 'long harbour' (Hakaroa in Southern Maori dialect). The little coastal settlements and roads are often named in French for the early settlers who arrived in 1840 only to find the British had raised their flag at Akaroa Harbour just five days before. Roads which radiate off the state highway may wind over high saddles then tortuously down to little bays, usually the site of early farming settlement. These roads can be very narrow, steep and shingled; on the south coast particularly they may end at farmsteads with no access to the sea. Several of these bays were headquarters for 'shore whalers' in the 1830s, harpooners who rowed off the beach in pursuit when a whale was sighted.

The hills have been largely cleared of timber but there are interesting forest reserves and public walks in some of the valleys, with others over high tussock-clad headlands above the sea. Much of the forest on Banks Peninsula was once totara with associated kahikatea and matai and broadleaf species. Near the peaks, surviving trees have been twisted and shaped by their exposure, forming a stunted goblin forest.

Distinctive birdlife of the remaining forest includes bellbird, brown creeper, South Island tomtit and native pigeon. New Zealand pipit range over the rough tussocklands while the endangered native falcon hunts overhead.

The wildlife of the harbours today includes New Zealand fur seals, common dolphins, and the largest surviving pods of Hector's dolphin, the world's rarest. The rocky coast is also a popular breeding ground for little blue penguin and yellow-eyed penguin (here at their northernmost limit). The volcanic reefs are often wrapped in the giant arms of bull kelp and the rockpools shelter southern species such as sea tulip.

HECTOR'S DOLPHIN

Variously known as the world's rarest, and the world's smallest, marine dolphin, Hector's are creatures of the South Island east coast. Only 1.2–1.4 metres long, the dolphins move in small family groups, their populations fallen from an estimated 26,000 in the 1970s to around 7400 often through set-netting. Local populations are endangered but can be seen from tour boats off Kaikoura, Akaroa and Otago Peninsula.

A separate population of a subspecies known as Maui dolphin ranges the waters from Taranaki to the Kaipara along the North Island west coast. Their numbers have dropped to around 100.

▼ *BELOW: Hector's dolphin, the world's smallest and rarest marine dolphin.*

LAKE ELLESMERE

Broad but shallow Lake Ellesmere lies on the Canterbury Plains on the south side of Banks Peninsula. Its presence is a reminder that the Waimakariri River once went to sea here, instead of to the north of Christchurch.

Extending over 278 square kilometres, Ellesmere is home to thousands of wetland birds. These affect the quality of the water, which is also enriched by run-off from surrounding farms. Thousands of Australian black swans nest around the fringes. Many of the 10,000–15,000 resident Canada geese migrate from here in spring to breed in the high country.

Only a narrow spit, built up by the longshore drift of boulders from southern rivers, keeps Ellesmere separate from the sea. Kaitorete Spit is more properly a continuous barrier stretching some 24 kilometres along the Canterbury Bight from Banks Peninsula, varying in width from 250 metres to 5 kilometres.

Kaitorete Spit is a refuge for several species of skink and gecko, and also has its own moths and shrub. The golden native sand-binder, pingao, survives extensively on the dunes along the spit. Tangled shrubs of the hip-high tororaro, *Muehlenbeckia astonii*, comprise most of the surviving examples of this rare species.

◀ *LEFT: Kaitorete Spit meets Banks Peninsula near Birdlings Flat. Here at Poranui it also retains waters from Lake Forsyth (also known as Wairewa or Kaituna, meaning eel food). Over its 24-kilometre length the boulder barrier of Kaitorete varies in width from 250 metres to 5 kilometres, some of it farmed, but the coastline is protected in reserves.*

Ellesmere is known aptly in Maori as Te Waihora — 'spreading waters'. It was a significant food source for old-time Maori, along with the adjacent Lake Forsyth (known as Wairewa or Kaituna — eel food), a drowned valley which tucks into the edge of Banks Peninsula. Migrating eels are still taken from these lakes as the fish cross the spit to the sea in January–April.

Birdlings Flat, between the two lakes, is a popular place for gathering semi-precious gemstones from the shingle deposits.

▲ *ABOVE: Looking south from the Summit Road near Gebbies Pass on Banks Peninsula. The waters of distant Lake Ellesmere/Te Waihora extend over 278 square kilometres. It is protected from the sea by a continuous barrier of shingle called Kaitorete Spit and surrounded inland by intensive farming. A major gathering place for birds, Lake Ellesmere was recognised in 1981 as a wetland of international importance.*

CANTERBURY
HIGH COUNTRY

The best of wild Canterbury can be accessed directly from pretty inland roads which run at the back of the Canterbury Plains, along the foothills of the Southern Alps. From here there are several possible excursions into the mountain valleys with their great braided rivers.

State Highway 73 runs inland from Christchurch and across Porters Pass into the tussock basins of Craigieburn, which are now largely preserved in a new drylands park. Beyond them lie the Southern Alps, where beech forests blend into the alpine forests of Arthur's Pass National Park. (Westland lies beyond.)

There are further roads from the plains, inland into the high country, exploring the courses of the great rivers. The road from the Rakaia Gorge runs inland to Lake Coleridge and beyond. The Ashburton rivers give access to the Ashburton Lakes district deep in the mountains. The Rangitata Gorge leads inland to the great sheep runs which inspired the Victorian satirist Samuel Butler to set his *Erewhon* novels there.

Burkes Pass from Fairlie leads by SH8 into the vast Mackenzie country, with its huge glaciated lakes, and the roads to Mt Cook and Central Otago.

▲ *ABOVE: In late winter and early summer these shingle areas are used as nesting places by thousands of ground-nesting birds, many of them migrants. In the foreground of this mossy patch beside the road is a banded dotterel.*

◀ *OPPOSITE: High-country braided riverbed. In this ever-changing environment tiny mat plants can spread across the shingle, along with colourful lichens and mosses. Willowherbs and other plants barely 5 cm high grow in colourful clumps. Many of the cushion plants are species of* Raoulia *which form yellowish-green patches on the shingle. Insect life is rich, attractive to birds that gather here to breed.*

These high-country regions are all drylands, starved of the rain which has been dropped instead on the other side of the Southern Alps. In this rain-shadow area some places receive less than 500 mm of precipitation a year, in contrast to 5000 mm west of the Alps. As the prevailing westerlies cross the Alps, dropping rain on Westland, they gather speed and heat, expressed in strong northwesterlies which blow to the east coast plains. On the braided riverbeds they raise plumes of dust which can fill the horizon down country.

The predominant vegetation of these drylands is tussock grassland, punctuated by patches of prickly matagouri scrub and fierce spires of speargrass or 'wild Spaniard'. Variety is found about their roots; subalpine herbs lie in the shelter of the taller vegetation. On damper mountain slopes there may be patches of beech forest. Fire has reshaped these wild places, however, removing early totara forest and eating into the slopes of the alpine beeches.

Mountainsides are generally scarred by shingle slides, sometimes the product of earlier overgrazing, or damage caused by fires started to freshen the pastures. The youthful nature of the underlying rock makes the mountainsides particularly vulnerable to erosion.

Snow and ice are still working on the unstable slopes of the Southern Alps, splitting open the young rock and hastening the continuous process of erosion. Mountain streams dash down gullies and rocky valleys, flooding quickly and as quickly subsiding. The main rivers still flow in skeins across stony beds following the broad U-shaped valleys originally carved by glaciers during the ice ages. Their glacial outwash has created the extensive Canterbury Plains.

▲ *ABOVE:* There are more than 30 species of the needle-sharp speargrass or 'wild Spaniard', found in tussock and subalpine country.

▶ *OPPOSITE, TOP: Lake Heron in the high-country basin of the Ashburton Lakes district. Such lakes and wetlands, lying in the valleys of former glaciers, are now important habitat for migratory wading birds, and unusual wetland birds such as the Australasian bittern and the southern crested grebe.*

▶ *OPPOSITE, BOTTOM: Prickly matagouri bush grows in tussock areas. A nitrogen-fixing plant, it may colonise disturbed land, for example slips.*

THE BRAIDED RIVERS

Braided rivers are named for their habit of running in a network of rapid streams, as skeins of water between unstable islands of shingle and stones. The rivers rise in the roots of the Southern Alps, fed by melting snow and remnant glaciers. The milky blue colour of the water is the product of glacial rockflour carried in suspension.

The braided rivers follow long broad valleys, created by ancestral glaciers which covered these mountains in the ice ages. Their cargo of boulders fills the bottom of their U-shaped valleys creating in places riverbeds 3 to 5 kilometres across. When their waters burst forth from the mountains, these rivers are still carrying glacial boulders which are the foundation of the plains.

The nature of the great rivers of the eastern South Island has changed radically with the development of farming. The rivers often run in broad unstable beds between cliffs of wind-blown loess or the shingle beds of their earlier courses. In summer, after the snowmelt in the alps, they run in low streams but a flood at any time may swell the waters till they run bank to bank. In this ever-changing environment tiny mat plants can spread across the shingle along with colourful lichens and mosses. In late winter and early summer these shingle areas are used as nesting places by thousands of

ground-nesting birds, many of them local migrants.

The shingle islands have in many places been overrun by exotic plants, particularly broom, lupin, willow and gorse. Introduced wildflowers also spread across vacant ground. The consequence is the loss of habitat for ground-nesting birds.

The presence of predatory mammals in the riverbeds further threatens the birds: wild cats, ferrets, stoats and weasels are obvious enemies, but so too are hedgehogs which eat the eggs of ground-nesting birds.

Many of the braided rivers are threatened by development. Plans to dam and divert them are frequently mooted. Massive power schemes have reworked the sources of the Waitaki River and water extraction for irrigation of the flatlands is another pressure.

Braided rivers are the natural habitat of several rare and endangered birds which migrate there to breed. The most famous is the wrybill, a plover with a beak that curves to the bird's right, enabling it to probe under stones for its insect food. The wrybill breeds in the high-country

▲ ABOVE: High-country basins fill with glacial deposits. Rivers wander across them in braids of water.

◀ OPPOSITE: Downstream from their high-country gorges, the rivers spread out across the plains created by millennia of erosion.

reaches of rivers from North Canterbury to the Makarora and Matukituki in inland Otago. Most congregate on the riverbeds of the Waimakariri, Rakaia, Rangitata and high-country Waitaki rivers. The birds nest through August till January when they return to the northern harbours.

Other migrants nesting on the riverbeds are South Island pied oystercatcher and banded dotterel, along with pied stilt.

In spring and early summer the islands in braided rivers are also used as breeding colonies by black-billed gulls and the rare black-fronted tern. With the exception of the stilt and South Island pied oystercatcher, which also breed on farmland and on lakeshores, these birds are all in decline as a consequence of habitat loss.

CRAIGIEBURN

Just an hour inland from Christchurch, SH73 enters the high-country grasslands of the Southern Alps. The road to Westland runs through a mosaic of public lands protecting the tussock high-country and extending to the alpine forests of Arthur's Pass National Park on the Main Divide.

The road enters the Korowai/Torlesse Tussocklands Park as it climbs Porters Pass and continues into a vast inland basin of drylands, past Lake Lyndon to Castle Hill. The extensive grasslands lie between two parallel mountain ranges fronting the Southern Alps. The protected area extends from the snow tops of the Torlesse Range at 1998 metres to the east, to the Craigieburn Range with its beech forests, rising beyond 2000 metres to the west. Only the floor of the basin is private farmland.

Castle Hill is a surprise. Extensive outcroppings of limestone mark the Kura Tawhiti/Castle Hill Conservation Area of 54 hectares. Several caves among the limestone tors served hunting Maori who in pre-European times sought kakapo in nearby forests. Faint charcoal drawings by early Maori may be detected among the rocks. Later European drovers found one cave large enough to shelter a thousand sheep.

Beside Kura Tawhiti ('treasure from a distant land') is an absolutely protected block of apparently bare earth. This is the Lance McCaskill Nature Reserve in which several rare plants are protected, among them the Castle Hill forget-me-not, a tiny sedge, and a limestone wheatgrass, plants peculiar to this kind of earth. These once grew in a prehistoric forest of Hall's totara long lost to fires.

The long tongue of limestone extends across the tussock basin to a point between two energetic rivers which are joined underground by Cave Stream, another reserve.

CASTLE HILL

Kura Tawhiti/Castle Hill Reserve protects substantial outcrops of limestone in the Craigieburn–Torlesse basin. The area was once clothed in a forest of Hall's totara but this was burnt in Maori times. The place is significant to Maori, who came here to hunt for the nocturnal ground parrot, the kakapo and other birds, in prehistoric times. Seasonal food parties from the east coast took kaka, kukupa (native pigeon), kiwi and ducks along with the Pacific rat, an animal now extinct on the mainland. Fittingly, the Maori name of Kura Tawhiti refers to 'treasure from a distant land'.

◀ OPPOSITE: Limestone country in the Craigieburn valley.

TUSSOCK

The natural ground cover in the eastern drylands is tussock. These gold and silver native grasses once carpeted most of the hills and the plains from Marlborough to Southland. Today examples are preserved in a chain of conservation parks being established in the high country.

Native tussocks belong to several species, each preferring a particular stretch of range land. For example, snow grass grows most widely above the snowline; red tussock grows on damp and boggy ground at lower altitudes.

Narrow-leaved snow tussock prefers the higher country, such as the exposed tops of Te Papanui Conservation Park in Central Otago. The original tussocks on the Canterbury Plains often grew to the height of a man, impeding progress across country. Both Maori and European settlers in their time burnt the tussocks to clear their paths. Later fires were lit to provide fresh shoots to feed sheep. The bottom of some high-country valleys are now clear of tussock, removed to grow pasture grass and crops for winter stock feed.

ABOVE: Lake Pearson lies below the inland wall of the Torlesse Range. The area is heavily eroded but further south is protected in the newly created Korowai–Torlesse Tussockland Park.

▶ *OPPOSITE, TOP RIGHT: An underground river links two streams running through limestone gorges at Cave Stream Scenic Reserve near Castle Hill. The cave is usually explored from the outlet end on Broken River, following a wet and twisting course for nearly 600 metres underground, before climbing up beside a 3-metre waterfall to the inlet on Cave Stream. It is the home of a rare spider known as the cave harvestman which feeds in the dark chambers for insects.*

▶ *OPPOSITE, BOTTOM: Limestone rocks at Castle Hill. Larger rocks contain shelters and caves.*

There are private farms, known as stations, carrying cattle and sheep, in the lower floor of the Craigieburn basin. The higher country of Castle Hill is, however, public land. Much of the Craigieburn Range has long been protected to counter erosion in the 4451-hectare Craigieburn Conservation Park. The beech forests and alpine tussocks here flow back to the boundary with Arthur's Pass National Park. In summer some service roads to skifields and lodges give access to high-altitude carparks.

On the valley floor, Lake Pearson lies in two halves barely joined together; it is the protected habitat of breeding southern crested grebes. Lake Grasmere and Lake Sarah are further high-country wetlands on the edge of the Waimakariri Valley. The highway follows the course of that ancient glacier until the Craigieburn Range closes with the tangle of the Southern Alps and the west-bound road enters the forests of Arthur's Pass National Park.

ARTHUR'S PASS
NATIONAL PARK

As the beech forests draw in on the upper Waimakiriri valleys, so they close about the mountains of the Southern Alps, and Arthur's Pass National Park. The Canterbury dry country turns into the wetland forests of the West Coast, or Westland, over a distance of just a few kilometres. The rainfall on the eastern edge of Arthur's Pass is about 1500 mm annually; on the West Coast side it is 5000 mm.

The route through the Southern Alps is made possible by Arthur's Pass itself, a 931-metre-high saddle in the otherwise barely broken line of the Main Divide. Goldminers and traders used the pass as access to the Westland goldfields in the 1860s. A railway tunnel was forced underneath it by 1923.

The geologically young mountains, still moving, have created bare tops and huge rockfalls into the forests. The swooping suspended curves of the highway into Westland are another measure of the challenges of this rough and changing country.

Arthur's Pass National Park was established in 1929, the first in the South Island. At 100,000 hectares it is just one section of the extensive mountain forests which follow the line of the Southern Alps both north and south of here. It is, however, far more accessible than the other forests that protect the headwaters of the other great southern rivers. People come here to walk in the alpine air and explore the varied plant life.

◀ *LEFT: Beech trees in Arthur's Pass.*

◀ *OPPOSITE, TOP: SH73 crosses the upper Waimakariri River to enter the forest vastness of Arthur's Pass.*

◀ *OPPOSITE, BOTTOM: Mt Rolleston (2271 metres), with its remnant glaciers, overlooks the Arthur's Pass road.*

On the drier eastern side of the Alps the beech forests predominate, containing mountain, red and silver beech. This thickens with undergrowth as the pass rises in the shadow of its highest feature, Mt Rolleston (2271 metres). The western rainforest begins just over the pass with a change to podocarp pines, and only occasional beech patches. The rich mixture of hardwoods includes rata (which flowers over Christmas), pink-and-white flowering kamahi, mountain toatoa and pahautea (the New Zealand cedar) plus a broad range of shrubs and small trees commonly found in rainforests.

Short walks include views of giant waterfalls near Arthur's Pass village. Nature walks include the Dobson, winding through montane plants close to the pass. Longer walks push up through the forest to the herbfields of the snowline. Emerge from the forest and find, at first, the windshorn bushes of tree daisies, dracophyllums, speargrasses and mountain flax; then the band of tussocks, which in turn shelter the tiny flowers of gentians, various mountain daisies, hebes and buttercups.

The mountaintops are the home of introduced chamois, a mountain goat from Europe, and occasional Himalayan thar, both grazing enemies of the fragile environment. Efforts to eliminate them are confounded by high-country farmers encouraging herds and selling access to mountains along the alps to hunting tourists. Red deer also damage the forests, eating out the undergrowth. Australian brush-tailed possums graze the foliage. Possums are responsible for the bare skeletons of their favourite food, the rata, rising above the canopy in many parts of Westland.

Birdlife, however, is rich in its variety. Among the rare or unusual are the rock wren which still survives

◀ TOP LEFT: *Local walks to waterfalls such as the Devil's Punchbowl are popular from Arthur's Pass village.*

◀ LEFT: *Near the top of Arthur's Pass a walkway gives an opportunity to explore the subalpine shrubland.*

in the open lands above the bushline. Great spotted kiwi may be heard calling to each other at night.

The sociable kea, the mountain parrot, swoops shrieking over the valleys from snowline to the village. The birds are so confident they approach visitors in the carparks where they can chew through rubber trim and attack fixtures on the cars. South Island kaka, the duskier forest parrot, also occur but are more secretive.

The beech forests are the home of yellow-headed parakeet, yellowhead and the tiny rifleman, which clambers up tree trunks looking for insects. More common species are pigeon, tui and bellbird, tomtit and the treetop-dwelling flocks of brown creeper.

Arthur's Pass can be accessed from either the Canterbury or Westland coasts, or worked into a figure of eight journey around the South Island.

▼ BELOW: *The mountain parrot, kea, is reputedly the most intelligent bird in the world. An unusual sight close up, the birds about Arthur's Pass seem fearless as they try to strip items from visitors' cars or take food off the plates of people eating at the village café.*

CURIOUS KEA

The kea is a bird of the mountainous high country, most easily seen about Arthur's Pass though they gather at skifield and glacier carparks too. Reputedly the most intelligent bird in the world, the kea seems here to have no fear of people. It has earned an unfavourable reputation for stripping the trim from cars and stealing unguarded items from picnic sites.

In nature, kea are largely herbivorous though some have a reputation for attacking dead or weakling sheep to get at kidney fat. For this reason they were shot for a bounty up to 1970 and not fully protected until 1986.

They nest in holes among rockfalls close to the snowline. Their 'kea' cry can be heard high up in the mountaintops, or they may be seen swooping over the forest. The birds associate in small groups.

The kea is related to the kaka forest parrot but does not have a population in the North Island.

MACKENZIE COUNTRY

The broad expanses of the Mackenzie Basin are more redolent of a continental country than of the narrowest part of the South Island. The Mackenzie country is a huge tussock grassland, a place of wild shingle rivers, flowing in braided fans fresh from the Southern Alps. The lakes through which the rivers flow occupy deep depressions left by the retreat of the glaciers after the ice ages. Over all the raw peaks of the Southern Alps stand snow-clad on the western horizon.

The Mackenzie Country is named for a Gaelic shepherd accused of rustling more than 1000 sheep and taking them into this unknown land in the early days of European settlement. (He was later acquitted and left New Zealand.) The broad rivers which flow across the basin, from 3 to 5 kilometres wide in some places, carry the melt of significant glaciers which still hang from the Main Divide of the Southern Alps.

The long lakes of Tekapo, Pukaki and Ohau lie roughly parallel between steep-sided ranges once the walls of huge glaciers falling from the Southern Alps. There are still glaciers at their headwaters along the Southern Alps. Shingle rivers then flow through a vast basin, scarred with blue canals and filled with the glacial outwash of the eroding mountains.

Farther south is the valley of the Ahuriri, which has no lake and flows directly from a bush-walled valley now owned by the State. Approaching Birchwood Station there are extensive wetlands, tarns, pools, and slow-flowing spring creeks. This is the place to look for waterfowl, including rare black stilt. Vehicles are banned

▲ *ABOVE: Three major lakes descend from the glaciers of the Southern Alps. Glacial flour colours Lake Tekapo blue.*

◀ *OPPOSITE: Typical tussock country on the Lindis Pass, southern entry to the Mackenzie Country.*

beyond the homestead, providing peace and foot access to the head of a valley with its source in the Southern Alps.

The tussock basin of the Mackenzie country was settled in the late 1850s into huge leasehold sheep runs. The landscape has since been modified by the extensive reworking of its rivers into a massive hydro-electric scheme flowing into the Waitaki River. The Ohau, Pukaki and Tekapo rivers are the main sources of the system, which includes bright blue canals and artificial storage lakes in the Mackenzie Basin (Lake Ruataniwha) and the vast Lake Benmore, flooding the course of the Waitaki River for 25 kilometres. Further downstream (on SH83 leading to the North Otago coast) are the Lake Aviemore and Waitaki dams along the course of a once-braided riverbed.

The tussock lands have been further altered in recent years with the introduction of irrigation, making it possible in some places to run dairy cattle on what was once dryland tussocks. The area has also suffered from the depredations of rabbits which last got out of control in the 1980s, converting thousands of hectares to near desert. The ground between the tussocks, once rich in subalpine plants and grasses, became covered with an introduced hawkweed or hieracium. Nothing would grow through it.

Pine trees have further modified some tussock landscapes, wildings planted by the wind from earlier commercial forests.

In an effort to recover some of the damage, the power generator has been helping to clear riverbeds of weeds, such as willow, which cover the places where endangered wading birds breed.

Colourful beds of Russell lupin, planted from the 1920s, are another introduced pest which takes over nesting areas of birds such as wrybill, banded dotterel, black-fronted tern, black-billed gull, pied stilt and oystercatcher.

▲ TOP: *Black stilt or kaki have a tenuous hold in the Mackenzie Basin.*

◀ OPPOSITE, TOP: *A bush walk from Lake Ohau emerges from the forest into a glacial cirque, containing a rich variety of subalpine and alpine plants.*

◀ OPPOSITE, BOTTOM: *The valley of the Ahuriri river leads to a bush-clad glacial valley now preserved for its high-country values. Lakelets, ponds and swamps along the river flats attract rare and unusual waterbirds.*

BLACK STILT

The most spectacular recovery project has been the captive-breeding and rearing of the endangered black stilt, or kaki, which is now restricted to this region. Once widespread on braided rivers elsewhere, the wild black stilt population had dropped to 23 when recovery programmes began in the early 1980s.

In 2000–1 there were only 39 birds in the wild but 67 chicks were raised in captivity at the Twizel Black Stilt Research Centre in the Mackenzie country. Kaki nests in the wild are disturbed by mammalian pests such as wild cats, ferrets, stoats and hedgehogs. With an imbalance of the sexes, kaki may also hybridise with the common pied stilt. A wild population of around 100 survivors is now protected by pest-control programmes on the riverbeds, and by breeding in captivity.

SOUTHERN ALPS

SOUTHERN ALPS

The spine of the South Island is a series of snow-covered mountains still rising from deep beneath the earth. Described by experts as 'young mountains', these impressive peaks, averaging 1700 metres high, run continuously for 500 kilometres as the Main Divide. They are still unstable, gouged by glaciation and scarred by moving shingle slopes.

The Southern Alps and their adjacent ranges began rising about five million years ago along a line known as the Alpine Fault. This axis of movement is the product of the collision between the Pacific and Indo-Australian continental plates. The mountains not only rise up to 10 mm a year but they also slide horizontally against each other along the fault, shifting laterally some 20–30 mm a year.

This shearing movement has been sufficient to shift the land on either side of the fault by some 480 kilometres, as evidenced by the Red Hills. This mineral-rich mountain block has been split in two by the fault and transported, leaving the Red Hill in Nelson and the Red Hills in South Westland (see page 174).

Geologists estimate that if the ancient mudstones and sandstones pushed up as ranges were not continually eroded they should have reached an altitude of more than 20 kilometres by now. Glaciation and erosion, however, trim their slopes, washing the rising peaks down glacier-cut river valleys and out onto the coastal plains.

The Southern Alps begin in Fiordland and run north to the Nelson Lakes district where they turn along the east-trending Wairau Valley and into the sinking ranges of the Marlborough Sounds.

NOR'WESTERS

The Southern Alps are a defining feature of South Island weather. Prevailing westerlies sweep in from the Tasman Sea, dropping huge quantities of rain as they climb the forested west-coast faces of the alps. Heated by that journey the drying winds then fall into a rain shadow on the eastern side of the alps. The hot winds create drylands in the high-country foothills and generate the warm blast of the nor'wester winds which are a frequent feature of conditions in the eastern South Island. Clouds of loess still rise on the riverbeds when the nor'wester blows.

OPPOSITE: Dawn breaks as the moon sinks over Mt Sefton (3151 metres). The mountain is the highest mountain in Westland/Tai Poutini National Park.

PAGES 230–231: Day's end on Aoraki/Mt Cook, viewed from the Red Tarns track behind the Hermitage Hotel.

AORAKI/MT COOK

The highest peak in the Southern Alps is now double-named Aoraki/Mt Cook because of its special significance to both Maori and other New Zealand communities. The mountain rises to 3754 metres just forward of the Main Divide between Canterbury and the West Coast, and is still in the geological process of mountain building. So young are these mountains, and so fractured the rock, that the shifting masses of the alps are heavily prone to erosion. In 1991, some 10 metres fell off the top of Aoraki/Mt Cook in a rock avalanche that spread up to 500 metres wide.

While the English name of Mt Cook is quickly traced to honouring the British circumnavigator Lieutenant James Cook, Aoraki has a more mystical association. In southern traditions the whole range of the Southern Alps is Te Katiritiri o Te Moana — the foam of the sea. When a heavenly canoe carrying the sons of Raki, the Sky Father, failed to take off from the ocean it overturned in the breaking sea. The canoe came to rest on its side, with the main peaks of the alps being the ancestors who clambered to the highest side and were turned to stone. The greatest among them is Aoraki, 'cloud in the sky'.

This country is surrounded by the mountains of the Main Divide, of which Mt Cook is the tallest and nearby Mt Tasman (3497 metres) the runner-up. In the 70,796 hectares of the park there are 19 peaks more than 3000 metres high. Some 40 percent of the park is covered in icefields and glaciers.

Closest to Aoraki/Mt Cook village is the Hooker Glacier descending from Aoraki between the Main Divide mountains and the Mount Cook Range. Stand at its terminal moraine and listen for the crash and boom of frequent avalanches in the adjacent gullies.

The Tasman Glacier, which descends on the other side of the Mount Cook Range, is New Zealand's longest at 27 kilometres. Its terminal lake is growing as the glacier gradually melts.

While tackling the mountains demands serious climbing skills, the environment of the Southern Alps is easily accessible around Aoraki/Mt Cook village. The alpine flowers and glaciers of Aoraki/ Mt Cook National Park have attracted

OPPOSITE: *The Hooker Glacier falls from the Main Divide of the Southern Alps and runs against the Mount Cook Range to become the Hooker River. This in turn joins the Tasman River flowing from the Tasman Glacier and into Lake Pukaki.*

MOUNT COOK LILY

This lily is actually a large white buttercup found in mountain tussock country along the Southern Alps. It was chosen early on as symbol of Aoraki/Mount Cook and used by pioneer tourist operators. Several large herbs add colour to the subalpine tussock lands. Other equally large mountain buttercups carry yellow flowers.

▲ *ABOVE: The white mountain buttercup popularly described as the Mount Cook lily.*

▷ *OPPOSITE, TOP: The peak of Aoraki/Mt Cook reduced by some 10 metres in a rock avalanche in 1991.*

▷ *OPPOSITE, BOTTOM: Lake Pukaki, below Aoraki/ Mt Cook, occupies the bed of an ancient glacier. The vivid blue of its waters is produced by glacial snow melt held in suspension.*

visitors for over a century. There are several short walks which provide an introduction to alpine flowers and meadows, and there is direct access to the face of the two great glaciers, the Hooker and the Tasman.

Walking in Aoraki/Mt Cook National Park provides a sampler of what may be found in more remote alpine regions. The iconic Mt Cook lily is actually a large white buttercup, just one of more than 300 different native plant species flourishing among the tussocks and rocks.

The forest patches are predominantly beech but there are interesting whipcord plants, such as hebes and dracophyllum, along with kanuka in the shrubby areas.

These high mountain valleys are the haunt of the alpine parrot, the kea, whose screech from on high is familiar to walkers. Kea often appear to be tame but can lift items such as camera cases or food from visitors in a matter of seconds. (See 'Curious kea', page 225.)

Other local birds include the pipit, bellbird, native falcon and, high in the alpine region, the tiny rock wren. Black stilt or kaki have natural habitat in the shingle bed of the Tasman River, which drains the major glaciers.

KA TIRITIRI O TE MOANA

To southern Maori the Southern Alps represent 'the frothing waters of the ocean'. The proud peaks are the surviving hull of a celestial canoe and its occupants.

Originally, the canoe of Aoraki came down from the sky carrying the first sons of the Sky Father, so they could see his new bride, the Earth Mother. Unsuccessful in their search, the four brothers sought to return to the heavens in their canoe, but a prayer to lift it from the water failed, and the canoe foundered on a reef.

When the canoe of Aoraki tipped up, the four brothers clung to its higher side. The canoe and its crew then turned to stone.

The tallest among them, Aoraki (cloud in the sky), remains as the tallest mountain in the Main Divide (Mt Cook). Others in Aoraki/ Mt Cook National Park include Rakiroa, the long Raki (known today as Mt Dampier); Rakirua, the second Raki (Mt Teichelmann), and Rarakiroa, the long unbroken Raki (Mt Tasman).

Subsequently named Mt Cook by a European navigator marking it from the Tasman Sea, this tallest mountain in New Zealand became the most sacred ancestor of the Ngai Tahu people of the South Island. Fittingly, the name Aoraki has now been restored. In the bilingual name, Aoraki/ Mt Cook, it now takes precedence over the historic English name, in recognition of the mountain's special significance to the people of the land.

THE LAST GLACIATION

Though ice ages occurred up to 2.6 million years ago, the shaping of New Zealand's South Island was substantially carved by the last glaciation, which ended only 11,500 years ago.

The fields of ice which carved into the Southern Alps ground out their U-shaped valleys and carried the waste downstream to form fans of coastal land such as the Canterbury Plains. Fine glacial sands, whipped up by the wind, topdressed the land, depositing beds of loess which form a large part of the eastern soils.

For a time, New Zealand's shores extended well out on the continental shelf as broad plains. Much of Cook Strait was a land-bridge then, linking the North and South islands. The melting of the ice, worldwide, created a new landscape. Sea levels rose dramatically, some 100–130 metres in places.

In New Zealand coastal mountains and their river valleys flooded, making islands of many higher ridges. The rising water filled the Hauraki Gulf, where ancestral rivers such as the Waitemata flowed eastward through forest into a down-faulted valley along the inner coast of Coromandel. In Marlborough the slowly sinking coastline was drowned by the incoming sea, creating the waterways and islands of the Sounds.

ABOVE: *Aoraki village is built on the glacial outwash of the Hooker Glacier, beyond.*

OTAGO

NORTH OTAGO

The self-styled White Stone City of Oamaru reflects the surrounding limestone country in its business quarter, built from this Oamaru stone. From Victorian Gothic to touches of Palladian and Classical, these buildings surround the old port precinct and raise their 'white stone' columns on the main street. Yet it is the remains of a basalt volcano, which rises on the southern edge of town, that begins the wilderness coast.

The bulk of Cape Wanbrow is a mass of volcanic material where lava has leaked under the sea and eroded, creating a dome of rock. Limestone and sedimentary rocks tie the uplifted volcano together. At its feet, tiny coves shelter bird colonies and often provide haul-out areas for seals.

An old stone quarry in the outer edge of the port is the breeding home of more than 100 little blue penguins. A small grandstand is built here so visitors can see the mass of birds returning to their burrows at nightfall, nearly 150 at peak season (the 2008 record was 275 birds). Follow the track from here round Cape Wanbrow and encounter fur seals, often swimming in the swirls of giant kelp which entangle the rocks. Pillow lava tubes, emerging in cross-section as round formations on the lower cliff faces, are evidence that underwater lava once flowed here in tubes like toothpaste.

A mixed colony of spotted and Stewart Island shags nest on the cliffs. In summer hundreds of both species of shag also crowd on the outer mole of Oamaru harbour and roost all over an adjacent wharf.

WAITAKI VALLEY

The North Otago coast begins south of the Waitaki River valley where the broad, braided river flows down from the Mackenzie country (page 226). Dammed into a series of hydro-electric power schemes, the river is largely tamed. Among the notable features of the valley are roadside rock drawings by pre-European Maori travelling to old hunting grounds.

A geological trail through the tributary valleys of inland North Otago and back down to the coast features fossil evidence of the past and a range of interesting limestone formations.

◀ OPPOSITE: A fur seal lounges where little blue penguins return to their colony at dusk.

◀ PAGES 240–241: Reefs and rocky shores are features of the North Otago coastline.

▲ TOP: *Yellow-eyed penguin.*

▲ ABOVE: *Little blue penguin, southern variant.*

▶ OPPOSITE: *Bushy Beach — a typical cove sheltering seals and yellow-eyed penguins at Cape Wanbrow, Oamaru.*

A road down the spine of Cape Wanbrow leads to cliffs over Bushy Beach where yellow-eyed penguins breed. Visitors can see the birds coming ashore to feed their young in the coastal shrubs, from around 3pm in the spring–summer breeding season. The young fledge in late summer and early autumn but the penguins continue to use the same coast year round.

The journey down the North Otago coast includes some spectacular seascapes and peninsulas. Winding roads run close to the sea but places of particular interest can be reached as side trips from the faster SH1.

Moeraki has spectacular round boulders along its beach. Some of these concretions are up to 3 metres through and have eroded out of the low cliffs which back the beach. They were formed around 60 million years ago under the sea, forming as accretions around scraps of bone, shell or stone. Maori regard them as calabashes and baskets of food washed ashore from their ancestral canoe Araiteuru, which foundered on this coast. Their evidence includes 'rope' strands of golden calcite crystals around the stones which gives the appearance of holding nets.

The nearby settlement of Moeraki is a fishing village with a lighthouse on a nearby peninsula. Here rocky coasts and cliffs provide shelter for nesting penguins and visiting fur seals.

Shag Point is a similar settlement, also with a lighthouse. Again yellow-eyed penguins frequent the beaches. Seals are sometimes joined by New Zealand sea lions, which are increasing along the North Otago coast. The remains of

a nineteenth-century industry which employed 127 miners have vanished, except for occasional beds of coal poking into the wild guts of the ocean reefs.

If there is plenty of time, and scenery is part of the experience, then the journey south to Dunedin can be varied with side trips to other coastal settlements and picturesque estuaries.

▲ *ABOVE: The Moeraki Boulders have been washed out of the adjacent cliffs. They are concretions formed around a core over millennia.*

◀ *LEFT: Golden calcite gives some rocks the appearance of nets and calabashes washed from the wreckage of an ancient Maori canoe Araiteuru.*

◀ *OPPOSITE, TOP: The Southern Ocean surges ashore at Shag Point. Once this was the site of an underground coal mine. Miners could hear the engines of the little coal steamers moving through the sea above them.*

◀ *OPPOSITE, BOTTOM LEFT: Spotted and Stewart Island shags rest on a coastal rock below Cape Wanbrow, Oamaru. The two species share a breeding colony on the cliffs above.*

◀ *OPPOSITE, BOTTOM RIGHT: Inland limestone hills attract rock climbers.*

OTAGO PENINSULA

Dunedin promotes itself as New Zealand's wildlife capital, probably with its eyes on the Otago Peninsula which walls in the long harbour on its south side. The remains of an ancient shield volcano which once buried the area, the peninsula protects the entrance of the harbour at Taiaroa Head. On this dramatic headland seabirds gather, notably the only mainland colony of northern royal albatross.

The gentle inner bays of Otago Harbour also shelter wildlife, including seals and dolphins. Tides drain up to half the shallow water in the harbour, exposing big areas for feeding birds. Enjoying the nature of the peninsula can involve taking local tours from Dunedin or Portobello.

The University of Otago offers a tour of its marine research laboratories and aquaria, which display the wilderness of the harbour. The facility, officially known as the New Zealand Marine Studies Centre and Aquarium, lies on the edge of the harbour, down a narrow shingle side road from Portobello.

The royal albatross colony at Taiaroa Head includes an information centre and there are conducted tours of the northern royal albatross breeding area. This is the only mainland colony of this bird; most breed on offshore islands of the Chathams group about 1000 kilometres northeast.

Birds gather there in numbers in October to prepare for nesting among the windswept tussocks. The colony itself can be closed to visitors during November but usually there is the opportunity to observe the birds from underground tunnels.

ALBATROSSES

Northern royal albatross or toroa have been distinguished from the southern species and breed on islands off the Chathams group, about 1000 kilometres northeast in the Pacific, and at Taiaroa Head. The first birds bred on these clifftops in 1938 and their numbers have grown slowly as offspring return to their natal site to breed. Parent birds usually breed only every two years.

The birds breed in the spring but the single chick cannot fly for about eight months. The young may return to their birthplace after three years or more but don't breed until they are six to 10 years, when they pair for life. There may be 100 albatross swooping over Taiaroa Head in the breeding season, but many of these are juveniles, and there may be only 25 breeding pairs.

◀ *OPPOSITE: The northern royal albatross breeds on Taiaroa Head.*

Nearby, and at several other points about the southern coast, there is also an opportunity to observe the lives of yellow-eyed penguins or hoiho. The birds come ashore in spring from mid-afternoon to feed their young but return ashore most nights throughout the year.

The waters about the peninsula are home to sea mammals too. Taking a wildlife cruise on the harbour (from Wellers Rock on the peninsula or from the city) reveals nature and wilderness close up. There are fur seals and New Zealand sea lions in the waters around Taiaroa Head, and among the visitors, elephant seals and leopard seals. Overhead swoop mated albatross and younger birds which frequent the colony for some years before breeding. The birds have a wingspan of more than 3 metres and use the exposed headland to launch their bulk into the wind.

Around the edge of the land are colonies of Stewart Island and spotted shag. One unexpected site visible from the sea is a nesting colony of royal spoonbill, a large white wading bird, which has

◀ *TOP LEFT: The patch of shrubs in the centre of this cliff on Taiaroa Head is the refuge of a breeding colony of royal spoonbills. The birds nest on the top layer, where their position keeps off robber gulls and other predators. They wade inside the harbour, sweeping the detritus for marine animals with their long, spoon-tipped bills.*

◀ *LEFT: Taiaroa Head shows in its rock layers just how complicated its volcanic history is. Cliffs, rising 60 metres around the lighthouse, appear to be overlain with dark basalt but at lower levels red scoria provides niches where shags and seabirds nest.*

established on the top of coastal shrubs where the birds cling to a cliff face above the ocean. Deeper water comes close to the entrance to Otago Harbour and the upwelling is a popular feeding ground for seabirds, including the marine shags. Several different petrels, shearwaters and mollymawks (now known as albatross) also visit. Among three species of dolphin, the rare and endangered Hector's dolphin also hunts here.

On the southern side of the peninsula, the road winds past two substantial tidal areas at Hoopers Inlet and Papanui Inlet. Both attract wading birds and waterfowl in significant numbers. As the tides change, swan, geese, ducks and heron gather. In summer migrant golden plover and turnstone may join common New Zealand coastal birds.

▲ TOP: *Otago Harbour runs some 22 kilometres from downtown Dunedin to Taiaroa Head. The waters are shallow, only 2 metres deep in places. Low tide exposes nearly half the harbour seabed.*

▲ ABOVE: *The Taiaroa Head lighthouse rises 72 metres above sea level. Northern royal albatross breed on the adjacent headland.*

THE
CATLINS

The southernmost corner of mainland New Zealand feels remote with its extensive forests and isolated beaches. Exploring the Catlins coast requires a good map, and a plan, for many of the best bits are on gravel side roads leading down to the coast.

It is an area to explore at leisure. The coastal beaches are frequented by seals and sea lions, including the occasional elephant seal or leopard seal up from the subantarctic. The remnant rainforests shelter a good variety of forest and wetland birds.

The trees include large native pines, such as kahikatea and rimu, often standing in swampy land, particularly around river mouths. A thick undergrowth of kamahi, wineberry, lianes and other small native shrubs can give the coastal forest a jungle look.

On more open ground, thick coastal scrub and beds of rushes withstand the southern storms. Inland of the main road there is mixed rainforest, beech forest and cleared hill grazing.

◀ OPPOSITE: *Changeable weather and shifting light near Curio Bay typify the Catlins coast. Penguins and seals are seen in the surf.*

▲ *ABOVE: The Nuggets at Nugget Point are on a side road from SH29. Rocks in the sea provide safe nesting places for birds.*

▶ *OPPOSITE: Purakanui Falls, a landmark just off the main road through the Catlins.*

FRONTIER COUNTRY

The Catlins is a corruption of the name of Captain Cattlin, an early whaler, who began the original timber industry in 1840. The names and adventures of a number of settlers, including sealers and whalers, are reflected in other place names. Chaslands Mistake recognises another whaler and sealer active on the southern coast from 1824. In following years, timber-milling and clearing forests for farms reshaped the dense forests. Proper forest protection was not achieved till the 1990s.

Alternating bands of soft and hard rock running in ridges down to the sea have produced a varied coast of giant cliffs and golden beaches.

The region's wild coast begins by leaving SH1 at Balclutha and joining SH29 on the Southern Scenic Route, heading for Owaka, the main township of the Catlins. A series of mainly gravel side roads, off SH29, lead to some of the Catlins' best wild places.

Nugget Point is an early option. These 'Nuggets' of hard rock stand in the sea just off a giant headland with a lighthouse built in 1862. The narrow path out includes vertiginous views onto rock platforms where seals and sea lions haul out.

Red-billed gull colonies top the wind-wracked Nuggets while colonies of shags brave the cliff faces. Sooty shearwaters also breed here. In an adjacent bay a bird-watching hide overlooks a beach where yellow-eyed penguins return in the late afternoon.

Coastal forest is recovering among the bracken with native bushes such as muehlenbeckia/pohuehue, fierce nettles

(avoid), koromiko, plantings of windswept totara and kanuka, all gradually suppressing the beds of introduced yellow lupin.

Surat Bay, named for a shipwreck in 1874, is known as a place where sea lions come ashore. Formerly known as Hooker's sea lion, this big seal has been renamed the New Zealand sea lion in recent years. It is an animal of the subantarctic islands. Sea lions are about twice the size of a seal and can be aggressive, particularly if approached from the seaward side or if they are sheltering pups.

Jacks Blowhole is an interesting feature approached by a walk across private farmland from Jacks Bay (closed September–October for lambing). High on a clifftop, in the middle of a field, is the outlet of a monstrous sea cave far below. In wild conditions, at high tide, the booming water penetrates 200 metres inland through a sea cave before spouting over the surrounding land.

Purakanui Falls are a landscape feature reached by a short bush walk. The water comes down from the bush in three steps before rushing to the sea.

SOUTHERN SCENIC ROUTE

The highway through the Catlins (SH29) is part of a broader route promoted by tourism interests to guide travellers from Dunedin to Lakes Manapouri and Te Anau, and Milford Sound, via Invercargill, south of Dunedin.

It first passes Lake Waihola, an extensive wetland rich in waterbirds, beside SH1. The specially managed Sinclair Wetlands lie west off the main road near Waihola.

The Catlins coast is accessed south of Balclutha with a tangle of side roads running down to beaches and river mouths. Roads are narrow, sometimes gravel, and need care and a good map to follow.

At the southern end of the Catlins there is access north across the plains through Gore to Raes Junction and into Central Otago.

The Southern Scenic Route, however, follows the Southland coast via Invercargill and is distinguished by lonely beaches and significant wetlands about the outlets of the rivers. The route then heads north to Milford Sound along the eastern edge of Fiordland National Park.

▲ TOP: *Tautuku Bay, backed with coastal rainforest, has interesting walks down from the road.*

▲ ABOVE: *New Zealand (previously Hooker's) sea lion frequent several Catlins beaches. A subantarctic animal, its numbers are multiplying here. These animals can lunge swiftly and should not be approached too closely.*

Papatowai offers walks through forest to where moahunters once camped by the river mouth.

Tautuku Bay is a spectacular sweep of beach and forest, running for about 5 kilometres. Among walks there are short tracks through this forest and wetland to the ocean beach. Lake Wilkie is a small lake in deep forest, with a view showing how wetland vegetation around its shore then develops into rainforest.

A boardwalk gives access through tidal fields of jointed rush across to the broad coastal reaches of the Tautuku River. This is the habitat of the fernbird. Listen for its peeping as birds call to each other through the reeds. Fernbirds occasionally make short flights, trailing their distinctive flopping tail of fine feathers.

Cathedral Caves require a low-tide walk. The giant caverns are a measure of the force of the sea along this coast.

CURIOUS FOSSILS

Curio Bay is worth its deviation. In the broad bay it is possible to see dolphins and seals racing along the surf line. The special attraction, however, is a fossil forest where the trunks of fallen trees and their stumps can be easily seen in the rock platforms when the tide is out. These are specimens from an ancient forest which has been covered and later exposed again by changing sea levels. The trees predate the evolution of flowering plants and are believed to be ancient relatives of the pioneer kauri and podocarp families. The fossils are dated at around 180 million years old (remember, New Zealand separated from the supercontinent Gondwana around 80 million years ago).

Seals and penguins also frequent this coast.

▲ *TOP: Cathedral Caves can only be visited two hours either side of low tide. A charge applies.*

▲ *ABOVE: The fossils of ancient trees exposed on the rock platforms at Curio Bay.*

STEWART ISLAND/ RAKIURA

STEWART ISLAND / RAKIURA

Stewart Island and its outlying islands buffer the subantarctic edge of New Zealand. While settlement dates back to pre-European times, and early whaling and sealing camps are still evident, it remains largely a wilderness: a place of rocky coasts or lonely ocean beaches, where forested headlands encompass long, sheltering harbours, and wandering rivers penetrate the wetlands. At its remote heart bare granite mountains lie surrounded by original forests.

While access to this region is open to all, it's by walking in the main. The road system on Stewart Island is restricted to a few kilometres around the only village, Oban, with its population of around 400: so don't ship the car.

Nevertheless, Stewart Island/Rakiura is New Zealand's third largest island. In some legends it is reputedly Maui's anchor stone from when he fished up the North Island. Most of the island had been in Crown reserves for a hundred years before Rakiura National Park was formed in 2002. It covers 85 percent of the island, some 157,000 hectares. The new park inherited a network of walking tracks, more than 280 kilometres in length, often carried across the notorious mudspots on wooden walkways. A tramp

around the island can take 10–12 days, but there are many shorter journeys and day walks.

The plant and animal life of Stewart Island is rich and diverse, with species varying through narrow bands of altitudinal change. They include rare and endangered plants not found elsewhere, notably *Gunnera hamiltonii*, one of the world's rarest plants, a sand spurge with only seven known specimens. Threatened birds include several subspecies peculiar to the island, and an offshore colony of the world's rarest parrot, the kakapo.

Strangely, there are no beech trees, the typical mainland forest type of the colder places of the South Island. Instead tall podocarps rise beyond the village and, with various hardwood species, dominate the inland forests up to the 300-metre contour. These provide homes for many birds, including the threatened Stewart Island weka, yellow-crowned parakeet,

ABOVE: Ulva Island, an open sanctuary for rare birds, and its marine reserve, lie in Paterson Inlet, close to the town of Oban.

PAGES 258–259: Off the beaten track, Stewart Island is a difficult wilderness.

South Island kaka, Stewart Island brown kiwi, brown creeper, tui and bellbird, and the Stewart Island robin.

The exposed coast is often fringed with thick shrublands of wind-shorn manuka, and salt-resistant plants such as hebes, the whipcords of dracophyllum, flaxes and leathery daisy trees (muttonbird scrub). The coastal birds include Stewart Island and other shags, kiwi, petrels and shearwaters, small bush birds and weka. On the rocks and beaches, fur seals, and the occasional sea lion and sea elephant, may come ashore.

At sea, albatrosses (some known locally

 ▲ *ABOVE: Huge sand dunes back Mason Bay, Rakiura National Park.*

as mollymawks) soar among the many petrels and shearwaters, gulls and penguins which frequent these waters.

The broad harbour arms and their rivers are habitats for wetland birds and freshwater native fish — 11 species of them. These rivers have traditionally been highways through the dense forests, attracting visitors inland. At higher altitudes, tussock grasslands and herbfields cling to the sides of granite mountains, including the exfoliating domes of Gog and Magog.

An isolated population of the New Zealand or red-breasted dotterel has abandoned its coastal habit of the mainland, nesting instead on herbfields and flying up and down the mountains to feed on the beach some 500 metres below.

Beaches along the west coast and invasive sand dunes are another interesting habitat. At Mason Bay sand dunes spread over more than a square kilometre.

The absence of mustelids (ferrets, weasels, stoats), bird-killing pests of the mainland, is one reason for Stewart Island's rich birdlife. Nevertheless, rats, wild cats, possums and dogs are a major threat to birds.

The fabric of the forest is further damaged by possums and populations of red deer, white-tailed deer and goats. White-tailed deer, found elsewhere in only one location (in Mt Aspiring National Park), are particularly fond of the hardwood understorey of the forest. Possums graze out their 'ice cream' species, and create holes in the forest canopy letting in the damaging sea winds and causing 'die-back'. Erosion follows.

Even so the forests are imposing, and their treasures are readily available for the public to enjoy.

Ulva Island is an open sanctuary featuring rare and endangered species. The forested island lies in Paterson Inlet, just over a low hill from Oban settlement. Like the nearby landscape, the 267-hectare island is dressed in big trees, including rimu, rata and kamahi, and in coastal shrubs and forest. Free-ranging populations of Stewart Island's special birds include Stewart Island weka, brown kiwi, parakeet and bush robin, along with rare southern species such as the kaka, South Island saddleback and yellowhead. An adjacent marine reserve protects the broader environment.

The coastal seas about Stewart Island are littered with rock stacks and rocky islands, some 170 in all. Around 60 percent are less than 5 hectares; fewer than 10 percent are more than 40 hectares. These are usually the haunt of seabirds, including huge populations of 'muttonbirds', titi or sooty shearwater, which are still harvested annually by their traditional Maori owners for sale on

SAVING KAKAPO

The last wild population of 61 kakapo was removed from the Tin Range on Stewart Island between 1980 and 1992 and secured on pest-free islands elsewhere. Kakapo, meaning night parrot, are flightless and one of the world's rarest birds.

A breeding population was established on Codfish Island (Whenua Hou) 3 kilometres to the southwest of Stewart Island after rats were removed in 1987. From Codfish, some birds have since been relocated to Anchor Island in Dusky Sound, Fiordland, as part of a recovery programme.

Breeding is erratic and numbers remained static for several years. (The total population was still only 62 in 2000.) Kakapo depend on the unpredictable fruiting of trees such as rimu to sustain breeding. Their subsonic mating calls can be heard up to several kilometres away. Successful breeding occurred in 2002, adding 24 chicks, and again in 2009 when some 34 chicks brought the population to 125.

The endangered Cook's petrel also breeds on Codfish, its only southern colony.

the mainland of New Zealand.

A particularly important island is Codfish, also known as Whenua Hou, managed as an absolute sanctuary. It is to here that the last kakapo, flightless ground parrots, from Stewart Island and Fiordland were taken during the 1980s in a bid to breed a bigger population in a pest-free sanctuary. The island is closed to the public, though a tame kakapo was shown at the open sanctuary on Ulva Island during 2006 and has since toured zoos.

There is a special atmosphere about Stewart Island, which lies in the Roaring Forties of latitude. The light is softer here on the edge of the subantarctic. Days are short in winter but night comes slowly in summer, the sinking sun lighting the southern sky till late in the evening. The magnificent sunsets and displays by the southern aurora may have given the island its Maori name of Rakiura, '(the isle of) glowing skies'. The original name of Rakiura was fittingly restored in 2002 to cloak the national park.

▲ *ABOVE: Charter planes land on the beach at Mason Bay, a broad area of sandhills where kiwi are sometimes seen hunting in daylight. Rare dune plants are protected while the area is being replanted with native pingao, a sandbinder, replacing introduced marram. An overland trek through wetlands and forest gives walking access back to Paterson Inlet with a boat ride to Oban.*

▶ *OPPOSITE, TOP: Tidal arm of the sea on the road north from Oban.*

▶ *OPPOSITE, BOTTOM: Forest grows to the saltwater in places such as Paterson Inlet.*

DAYTIME KIWI

Stewart Island's brown kiwi, or tokoeka, have developed the peculiar habit of feeding by day. A nocturnal bird in the rest of New Zealand, brown kiwi on Stewart Island may be seen probing for marine organisms in daylight along the great ocean beach at Mason Bay, and elsewhere. There are reputedly 25,000 kiwi at large on the island. They belong to the same species as those about Haast and Fiordland but those feed only by night. Guided trips to see kiwi are available from Oban.

FIORDLAND/
TE WAHI POUNAMU

FIORDLAND/
TE WAHI POUNAMU

The tangle of mountains which make up the southwestern corner of New Zealand have been largely shaped by ice. Fiordland was likened by Maori to moko, its topography resembling the patterns of tattoo carved into the land by the demigod Tu te Raki Whanoa.

Only partially explored till the introduction of helicopters, the region makes up New Zealand's largest national park at more than 1.2 million hectares. The jumbled landscape of tall mountain blocks, separated by U-shaped valleys and fiords, is the product of glaciations over the past two million years.

Road access to this rugged landscape is limited, though the region hosts some of the greatest walks in New Zealand. The mountains rise westward of the Southland plains, edged by glaciated valleys and lakes, including bush-bound Lake Hauroko, the deepest in New Zealand at 462 metres, and Lake Te Anau, large enough to have its own branch glaciers and fiords carved from deep within the mountains. Here, at the eastern fringe of the park, annual rainfall is 1200 mm a year — it rains 200 days a year in Fiordland — while the western fiords take the brunt of the Tasman storms with 8 metres of rain recorded annually at Milford Sound.

In the narrow confines of the 14 fiords, the mountains have sheer walls, falling a thousand metres and more, from the snowy tops into deep valleys now flooded by the sea. These fiords are places of dark forest, heavy rain, wet rock and waterfalls. Their peace is often disturbed by the sudden fall of katabatic winds from the alpine tops — caused by temperature inversion — and equally sudden parades of waterspouts swept up in an instant from the surfaces of the confined seas.

Silver beech forests along the valley walls cling to a shallow layer of humus and moss, sometimes slipping down in vertical patches as an avalanche of forest. Silver beech is the most common tree but native pines such as totara and rimu grow with tangled undergrowth on lower land formerly planed over by the glaciers.

In high parts of Fiordland the rainfall may be around 17 metres a year. Giant waterfalls are joined by many more as the rain sets in. The rainfall is such that the saltwater in the fiords lies under a permanent surface layer of tannin-rich freshwater some 3 metres deep.

This semi-opaque layer creates a dark habitat close to the surface with forests of black coral, sea pens and other deepwater species in the first 40 metres. In this comparatively warm water some seven million colonies of black coral trees have been recorded, the largest concentration in the world.

The fiords themselves are also deep, their walls continuing straight down underwater from the sheer valley sides. Miles from the open sea on Long Sound, and only metres from the shore, the depthfinder records that the bottom is

▲ TOP: *Moss swamp in the shelter of beeches on the Milford Track.*

▲ ABOVE: *The Darran Ranges overlook the Hollyford Track.*

undetectable, lying somewhere below the instrument's working limit of 180 metres depth.

Those who want to see the landmarks of Milford Sound have the option of a long, twisting drive, or a four-day tramp over the Alps by the celebrated Milford Track. Other classic tramps in the park include the Hollyford Track, tramps in the Routeburn area bordering Mt Aspiring National Park, the Kepler Track above Lake Manapouri, and the Hump Track in the southern forests. More difficult to access is Doubtful Sound, involving a voyage across Lake Manapouri, a bus trip over the Wilmot Pass then a boat trip on the Sound itself. Charter trips are the only way to explore the wilderness of the southern fiords, including the landmarks recorded by James Cook during his visits there in 1773. Sealers and whalers followed his charts, building temporary settlements there in the 1790s. Only in recent years have the fur seal populations begun to recover. Dolphins of various species are also a feature of the coast.

Fiordland has its own penguin, the threatened Fiordland crested penguin, as well as the more common little blue species, and yellow-eyed penguins. Birdlife in Fiordland, however, has suffered a sore blow from the devastation of rats, possums and other pests.

Some of the offshore islands have been used in recent years to create pest-free habitats, with the endangered kakapo liberated on Anchor Island, and the South Island saddleback restored to Fiordland at Breaksea Island. Further refuges are being established on Secretary and Resolution islands.

The public opportunity to see such

TE WAHI POUNAMU — SOUTH WEST NEW ZEALAND WORLD HERITAGE AREA

New Zealand's southwest is recognised internationally as one of the world's most outstanding natural areas. Created in 1990 by UNESCO, the World Heritage Area extends earlier recognition of Fiordland, Aoraki/Mt Cook and Westland/Tai Poutini as national parks. It now covers intervening lands including Mt Aspiring National Park. Altogether Te Wahi Pounamu covers 2.6 million hectares, some 10 percent of New Zealand's land area.

The Maori name refers to the region as 'the place of greenstone', a highly valued jade.

Te Wahi Pounamu meets all four guiding criteria for international recognition. These include showing: the major stages of earth's evolutionary history (glaciation, and links with the ancient super-continent of Gondwana); significant ongoing processes of geological and biological evolution; exceptional natural beauty; and significant natural habitats for threatened plants and animals.

◀ OPPOSITE, TOP: *Mitre Peak at the top of Milford Sound.*

◀ OPPOSITE, BOTTOM LEFT: *Looking down the 'twelve second drop' from the top of Mackinnon Pass onto the next hut 970 metres below.*

◀ OPPOSITE, BOTTOM RIGHT: *Hidden Falls on the Hollyford Track.*

birds, however, is limited to Te Anau Wildlife Centre, which displays rare birds that may have been injured or involved in a captive-breeding programme. Most spectacular is the takahe or notornis, which was believed extinct for 50 years before its rediscovery across the lake from Te Anau, in the Murchison Mountains, in 1948. While it is possible to visit the Te Anau-au Caves, at the bottom of this massif, the Mt Murchison Takahe Special Protected Area is closed to the public to protect a falling population of less than 100 birds which live in the tussocks around the snowline.

▲ TOP: *Seals frequent the rocky shores of the fiords.*

▲ ABOVE: *In the sheltered waters of Dusky Sound, Fiordland.*

▶ OPPOSITE, TOP: *The classic U-shaped valleys carved by glaciers. Flooded, they form fiords.*

▶ OPPOSITE, BOTTOM: *The course of the Milford Track, up the Clinton Canyon to its crest here at Mackinnon Pass.*

MILFORD TRACK

Described for more than century as 'the finest walk in the world' the Milford Track is the most popular challenge in Fiordland. The track, from Lake Te Anau to Milford Sound, crosses the Southern Alps, traversing two huge glacial valleys through dense beech forest . The journey covers nearly 54 kilometres, and up to 18 kilometres in a day. The route over the Mackinnon Pass climbs in a zig-zag to 1069 metres.

The Department of Conservation offers communal lodges for 'freedom walkers' in parallel with privately owned lodges including luxury accommodation. Bookings for both are essential.

Other similarly managed tracks include the Routeburn, the Greenstone and the Hollyford.

CENTRAL OTAGO

CENTRAL OTAGO

Behind Dunedin, and stretching back to the Southern Alps, lies Central Otago. This interior of Otago is radically different from the surrounding alps and coastlines. Likened to a desert in places, its mountains may be buried in snow at midsummer while, at the same time, valley temperatures are among the highest in New Zealand.

At its core Central Otago is a series of parallel schist ranges with romantic names often reflecting their appearance — the Rock and Pillar, the Knobby and Raggedy Ranges, the Old Man and the Old Woman Ranges — with their distinctive rock tors rising from their tops and ridges.

In primeval times this landscape was eroded into a flat plain, sunk, then raised again into what is known as a 'denuded peneplain'. Rivers have since cut that countryside into mountain ranges, blocks of stone with rivers in between.

Most of the hill country is still planed relatively flat so that up there the views lie across extensive tussock country, with rolling downs, mires and occasional tors — resistant rock stacks that punctuate the skyline.

The valleys are generally broad, the rivers often incised in rocky gorges, and the adjacent land varying from gravel outwash from the ice ages to riverine deposits. The Taieri River is the wandering exception, at one stage entering into a sinuous series of bends, as it slowly snakes down Strath Taieri.

Widely worked over for gold in the nineteenth century, the mountains and the valleys between show frequent signs of pioneer industry. Ruins of the old miners' huts, built from clay and local stone, still stand in places such as Fruitlands in the Clutha Valley. Cliffs of clay mark where monitor hoses washed into river terraces to release gold-bearing deposits. Other ruins stand on the uplifted hills where spoil heaps, mine holes and crushers indicate where later industrial miners sank shafts to reach the gold reefs. Then there are the extensive spoil piles, known as 'tailings', left behind by dredges working along the boulder riverbeds in the first half of the twentieth century. Since then, farming has marked out orchards, sheep stations, and vineyards known best for their pinot noir and sauvignon blanc.

The rivers, such as the rolling blue Clutha and its contributors, are farmed to their banks, but the banks and roadsides are coloured with extensive patches of introduced weeds.

Among them are dog rose with its autumn crop of rosehips adding colour to the stone outcrops. On stony land near Alexandra the tiny biting stonecrop grows in huge patches like a yellow scab. Wild thyme grows in extensive areas, a plant once gathered for the catering trade but now left to the bees. Purple vipers bugloss and the yellow spires of woolly mullein add seasonal colour, as do the multicoloured spires of Russell lupin. Yellow broom and gorse occupy conspicuous corners on rough ground.

Poor farming techniques and lack of water are given as causes of the collapse

▲ TOP: *From a reserve above the Taeiri Plain; tussock and hebes protect the hillsides.*

▲ ABOVE: *Schist rocks pierce the tussocks at Salt Lake Reserve.*

SCHIST ROCKS

The rocky tors which cap the hills and some valley sides in Central Otago are made of multi-layered siltstones called schist. Laid down under the sea more than 200 million years ago, they were then compressed (metamorphosed by heat and pressure) and uplifted. The name schist reflects the Greek word to 'split', as it easily does, in layers.

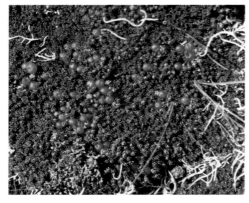

▲ TOP: *The remains of miners' huts dot the landscape. Explore ghost towns such as Welshtown and Logantown above old Bendigo, sites of hard-rock tunnelling.*

▲ ABOVE: *Look between the tussocks for a rich variety of subalpine plants.*

of wilderness but the introduction of rabbits in the nineteenth century was largely blamed for the deterioration of native cover. The rabbits reached plague proportions before stoats were introduced to control them. These mustelids soon moved on to native birds.

Central Otago is beautiful but no longer part of native wild New Zealand. The most significant trees following the courses of rivers and streams are introduced willows and poplars, a soft green contrast to the rocky hills in spring and summer, a band of golden foliage in autumn, then skeletons frozen by hoar frost against the winter snows.

The truly natural world of Central Otago is contained largely on the tops of the ranges, the original uplifted 'plains'. Here tussock grasslands prevail. Also in the grasslands are hebes and the spiny carrot-relative wild Spaniard, or speargrass, of which there are some 30 species in New Zealand.

On the exposed tops only windswept plant communities can retain the surface of the land. The association of miniature shrubs and subalpine herbfields makes the surface a multicoloured patchwork. Some of the plants are less than 30 cm high but their age can be as much as 200–300 years.

Animals that live at this altitude include moth and butterfly species adapted to living among the tussocks. A weta (a large native grasshopper) survives the seasons of snow because its blood contains glycol which stops it freezing.

Another of the natural treasures living among the rock stacks are giant lizards peculiar to this region.

Native pipits flourish in the tussock-land. There are also chukor, a gamebird introduced from India. The native falcon is a natural predator, hunting over the tussocks.

This was once totara and matai forest but it burned with the arrival of moa-hunting Maori and their successors. Occasional remnants of this forest can be found, usually in the form of stumps and logs or in the bottom of sheltered gullies where the fires did not reach.

In recent years, a campaign by conservationists and fish and game groups has persuaded governments to work on a network of upland and grassland parks. These include more than 20,000 hectares on the shoulders of the Old Man Range and the Lammermoor Range as the Te Papanui Conservation Park. Some six other grassland reserves are being sought.

The opportunities to explore these upper

▲ *ABOVE: Wild thyme grows widely on the rocky hillsides of Central Otago. The herb was once the basis for an industry which has spread of its own accord.*

DRIEST LANDSCAPE

High above the gorge containing Lake Roxburgh, the Flat Top Hill conservation area is a regenerating example of an extremely dry habitat. Lichens and scabweed covered the driest areas. In the 1860s this was a goldfield, and subsequent farming exhausted the land, which was overgrazed and infested with rabbits. Since reservation in 1992, native species have returned, overtaking the invasive thyme and other weeds, in a process which it is hoped will re-establish native tussock and shrubs. Flat Top Hill is in a rainshadow area, 6 kilometres south of Alexandra, and has an annual rainfall of only 300 mm. Despite this more than 182 different species of native plants have been recorded there.

Schist rocks or tors dot the landscape of the ranges. The snow- and wind-shorn meadow of native plants includes species 200–300 years old.

GIANT LIZARDS

Central Otago has the last populations of two giant lizards: the Otago skink at 300 mm long and the grand skink at 230 mm. Both are classified as 'nationally critically endangered' with their populations shrunk to around 2000 of each species. Their habitat is the high tor country, the rock piles of schist which mark the rolling uplands. The lizards' highly patterned backs blend with the lichen-patched rocks. Their Maori name, mokomoko, reflects these tattoo-like markings. The lizards don't hibernate even when snow covers the high country. Instead they hide in crevices in the rock and come out when the sun shines. Their diets include insects and the small berries of alpine plants.

lands by vehicle are few; what public tracks there are demand four-wheel-drives. Yet there are several walking tracks up the slopes of the ranges to public land. Because these are at various stages of development it is best to get up-to-date access details from the Department of Conservation.

The Cromwell cockchafer beetle has its own special reserve near the town. The species is restricted to an area of less than a hectare and was threatened by an expanding rubbish dump.

▶ OPPOSITE: *The Kawarau River rises from Lake Wakatipu and rushes to join the Clutha flowing through Central Otago. Early miners used to jump across at the narrowest point, though it is said to have eroded somewhat since then.*

SOUTHERN LAKES

SOUTHERN LAKES

The southern lakes of inland Otago bear the distinctive form of vanished glaciers that once ran down from the icefields of the Southern Alps. On their way to the now tussocked edges of Central Otago, the glaciers gouged out lakebeds, overrode smaller mountains and striated the valley walls with the scars of their passing.

Now filled by meltwater, these glacial lakes form a common catchment for New Zealand's largest river, the mighty Clutha. Their higher sources may lead to river systems which rise in the surviving glaciers of Mt Aspiring National Park.

AN INLAND TIDE

Lake Wakatipu has the phenomenon of its own tide or seiche. In places the surface rises and falls up to 12 cm. The frequency of the 'tide' is governed by the shape of the lake and the surface pressure, and is as little as five minutes in some places. A standing wave carries the seiche down the lake but this lineal movement is upset by transverse waves from the shores causing variations. Scientists suggest it is the product of the depth and pressure on the contained water due to atmospheric or wind variations. Test for the variation by putting a stick into the lakebed and see the water level rise and fall.

Wakatipu is the largest of the lakes. Its depth is such that its bottom lies 89 metres below sea level despite its surface elevation of 310 metres. Shaped like a figure Z it runs 80 kilometres through the mountains, from Kingston in Southland, around a deep turning at Queenstown, and up to Glenorchy in the Otago mountains.

Maori tradition tells of the giant Matau who slept in the mountains through the hot, dry winds. He stole a woman whose relatives set out to capture him. Matau was found curled in sleep among the mountains where he was secured and burnt. This gave the lake its folded Z-shape and left the beating heart deep below, causing the rise and fall of the surface water.

Among the raw mountains, the Remarkables overlooking Queenstown are among the best known, running in a ridge more than 2000 metres high to continue the lake shore of the Hector Mountains further south. The region is well known for its skifields.

Some ski roads in summer give easy vehicle access to subalpine fields of snow tussock, hebes, spaniard and other alpine plants. There are kea in places, the endemic pipit flies overhead, and the small bush falcon hunts the valleys and open country. In turn the lake is home to black teal (New Zealand scaup), a range of other ducks and Canadian geese.

Road access includes the lakeside drive to Glenorchy at the inland head of the lake. Here the Rees and Dart rivers provide walking access to the beech forests and the eastern edge of Mt Aspiring National Park. Another remote experience is to explore the deep gorge of the Shotover River, or the mining ghost towns, by off-road vehicle tours.

The Queenstown region was a centre for goldminers in the 1860s and the modern trend to build in schist combined with corrugated sheeting still gives the feeling of those early days of stone huts roofed in corrugated iron.

The extensive Arrow basin, dotted with shorn-off hills and glacial deposits, is widely subdivided in the area from Queenstown (soon to be a city) and Arrowtown. Autumn colour is provided by introduced trees, particularly willows and poplars which crowd the streamsides and landscape of Lake Hayes and Arrowtown. The particular attraction of the Queenstown region is the dramatic landscape rather than its wildlife.

Lake Wanaka is the next 'southern lake', to the north of Wakatipu, and over the Crown Range. This road, once notorious for its shingle climb to 1121 metres, 'the highest road in New Zealand', is now sealed. It still requires chains in snowy conditions. The road follows down a tussocked valley through Cardrona and into the extensive farmlands of the Wanaka basin.

The views are extensive from the town of Wanaka on the eastern lakeshore. The expansive horizon is filled with peaks from the Southern Alps at the far end. Lake Wanaka is 45 kilometres long and again its bottom descends through its

▲ *ABOVE:* Deep gorges and rushing rivers typify the wilderness in the Queenstown–Arrowtown district. A tourist jet boat explores the Shotover River, scene of an early gold rush.

◀ *PAGES 282–283:* The upper reaches of Lake Hawea run parallel to Lake Wanaka where the Haast Pass route crosses the 'neck' between them.

NEW ZEALAND'S HIGHEST ROAD

In addition to the road over the Crown Range there are two other claimants to the title of the highest public road in New Zealand, both 4WD seasonal routes. The Island Saddle, at 1400 metres, is on the electricity access road through Rainbow Station, east of Nelson Lakes National Park. The saddle into the Nevis Valley — south from Bannockburn in Central Otago and below the eastern wall of the Remarkables Range — climbs to 1300 metres, crossing the Carrick Range.

▼ *BELOW: Looking over the tourist resort of Queenstown at the Remarkables Ranges. Skifield roads give access to several subalpine environments when the snow melts.*

glacial origins to more than 30 metres below sea level. Among the shorebirds are endangered black-billed gulls, slender cousins of the common red-billed gulls. Among the ducks are the New Zealand scaup or black teal.

To get into the mountains, an unsealed road runs west up the lake and into the Matukituki Valley, revealing an unfolding series of snow-clad peaks in Mt Aspiring National Park. As the road approaches the Southern Alps, vast beech forests begin to replace the raw glaciated hillsides. Eventually the boundary of Mt Aspiring National Park and its track systems is reached under an amphitheatre of snowclad peaks.

The flatland in the broad valley of the Matukituki River is frequented with rough-country birds, including wrybill which nest here. Other birds frequenting the valley floor include the internal migrants, pied stilt and South Island pied

▲ *ABOVE: A placid Lake Wanaka from The Neck where Wanaka and Hawea practically meet on the Haast Pass road.*

oystercatcher, which breed here in late winter and early spring. The black-fronted tern 'hawks' insects over the paddocks and streams. Hunting falcon sweep over the rough land where spur-winged plover and banded dotterel also nest.

The Matukituki River contributes its waters to Lake Wanaka and the Clutha River leaves the lake near the town. The Clutha shortly swallows the combining waters of the Kawarau from Wakatipu and its subsequent contributors, the Shotover and the Arrow. Waters from neighbouring Lake Hawea run only 3 kilometres before joining the Clutha as it gathers strength and rushes eastward into Central Otago, bound for the sea.

Lake Hawea, which runs back to the mountains and the Hunter River, is 35 kilometres long. Again its origin is a giant glacier which has ground much of its mountain walls to shingle slides and bare faces.

Hawea has an uncertain shoreline. Artificially raised in 1958 for the generation of electricity it now has a regime of controlled levels. The variation of 18 vertical metres has given the foreshore a series of boulder terraces variously exposed depending on storage levels.

Despite this despoliation, the lake offers widespread mountain views from the road above its shores. This road eventually

▲ TOP: *Mountain ranges fill the view from the Lake Wanaka waterfront.*

▲ ABOVE: *The access road to Coronet Peak skifield exposes the course of the ancient Wakatipu Glacier.*

crosses the narrow 'Neck' to run further up the shores of Lake Wanaka. This route is another access to Mt Aspiring National Park, by way of the Makarora Valley, and eventually over the Haast Pass into Westland (see page 293).

CLUTHA/ MATAU-AU

Judged to be the second-longest river in New Zealand, the Clutha is measured as rising in the Mt Aspiring National Park by way of the Makarora River. This flows into Lake Wanaka and, by the time it reaches the sea south of Dunedin, the Clutha has run for 338 kilometres. That is only 16 kilometres less than the Waikato, the longest river (page 140) but by volume the Clutha is easily New Zealand's largest.

The river has had several names. James Cook named it the Molyneux; Clutha is a later Gaelic name translated from Scotland's Clyde.

A 1990s Maori claims settlement, seeking cultural redress under the Treaty of Waitangi, has restored the name of Matau-au, so that it now appears on many signboards as Clutha/Matau-au. The Maori name recalls the legend of the giant Matau who was burned in the bed of Lake Wakatipu (see page 284).

▲ TOP RIGHT: The Clutha River rapidly gathers volume from neighbouring lakes and contributing rivers.

▲ ABOVE: The Glenorchy road follows the northern arm of Lake Wakatipu giving access to Mt Aspiring tracks.

MT ASPIRING
NATIONAL PARK

At the centre of the World Heritage Area in New Zealand's southwest is Mt Aspiring National Park. Its huge and rugged terrain, its mountain slopes, beech forests, gorges and glaciers are remote from the experience of most people as roads penetrate only a few outer valleys. Its 355,000 hectares simply fills in the wild gaps between the other southern national parks: Aoraki/Mt Cook, Westland/ Te Poutini, and Fiordland.

The predominant forest is beech; red on the warmer, wetter slopes, silver and black/mountain beech in the colder valleys and higher in the mountains. Above the snowline, at 2000 metres, the mountains are trimmed with snow tussocks and herbfields to be buried in winter snow. This is where the tiny endangered rock wren makes its home among the boulders, surviving in crevices in the rocks when it snows.

Mt Aspiring National Park is best known to trampers who follow its Routeburn, Rees–Dart and Caples Greenstone tramps. Serious mountaineers may tackle its dangerous and isolated peaks. Among its remotest areas is the vast Olivine Ice Plateau, a declared wilderness area, where glaciers and snowfields merge in a caucus of peaks. A quarter of the park is here in a 50,000-hectare wilderness; remote, difficult of access, trackless and closed to aeroplanes.

Hidden in the heart of the park lies Mt Aspiring itself at 3033 metres. It is New Zealand's highest mountain beyond the bounds of Aoraki/Mt Cook. The Matterhorn-like summit can be glimpsed from signposted spots along the Matukitaki River road. The peak has been carved to its arresting spire by ancient glaciers which have cut back into the mountain mass from three sides.

Despite its size the park is accessible from the road in only a few places, serving instead as a magnificent mountain backdrop to the southern lakes from Wakatipu north to Wanaka and Hawea.

The park and its most famous walk abuts Fiordland National Park in the south where the Routeburn Track actually crosses the boundaries of the two

▶ *OPPOSITE: The Blue Pools on the Makarora River, in Mt Aspiring National Park, are a short walk from the Haast Pass road.*

parks. The bulk of Mt Aspiring National Park runs north from the Fiordland park boundary at the remote Humboldt Mountains. The park approaches the northern arm of Lake Wakatipu, its beech-lined valleys accessible by road via Glenorchy. Jetboat trips into the mountains penetrate some forested valleys such as the Dart.

Further access to the borders of Mt Aspiring National Park lies in the north via the vast Matukituki valley from Wanaka. A back-country road penetrates the front mountains to reach a view of the Southern Alps and the shingle riverbeds fed by snowfields and shrunken glaciers.

The northern face of the park is mostly experienced as a view from the highway which links inland Otago with the West Coast. Heading up the grass valley at the head of Lake Wakatipu to Makarora, the beech walls of the park begin to clothe the U-shaped valley. Short roadside walks penetrate the forest edge, including to the Blue Pools where the virgin river runs with glacial milk. Tracks and jetboats enter by the Wilkin River (from Makarora settlement).

The main road enters the forest beyond Makarora, rising along the northern boundary of the park to Haast Pass and the Gates of Haast. The spectacular rainforest route over the Haast Pass runs down into Westland, following the huge rock tumbles of the Haast River.

TITITEA

The Maori name of Mt Aspiring is Tititea; variously translated as the 'shining' or 'glistening one'.

◀ *OPPOSITE, TOP: The Matukituki River road from Lake Wanaka gives access to the ranges of the Mt Aspiring National Park.*

◀ *OPPOSITE, BOTTOM: Undisturbed native tussock on a Wanaka roadside.*

▼ *BELOW: Beyond Makarora the Haast Pass road enters beech forest which crowds the road.*

WESTLAND

SOUTH WESTLAND

Exploring the West Coast is a journey in itself. The road along the coast winds beside forests for much of its length — only 100 kilometres or so less than the journey from Wellington to Auckland.

On the way it touches on huge stretches of forest lying along the western edge of the Southern Alps. In places it clambers round mountainous bluffs high above the Tasman Sea, and elsewhere negotiates the edges of extensive wetlands, estuaries, lakes and fierce rivers.

Two living glaciers in Westland/Tai

Poutini National Park, and striking landforms such as the curious Pancake Rocks at Paparoa National Park (page 305), are highlights of a minimum two-day journey up the Coast.

Farthest south is the fishing village of Jackson Bay, 44 kilometres down a side road from Haast. Such isolated settlements were linked by the Haast Pass to Otago before a road up the West Coast was opened in 1965. Cook called this locality Open Bay; the Open Bay Islands, 4 kilometres offshore, were once the site of a sealing industry. In the 1810s, a sealing crew was castaway on an island for three years before rescue. They had killed 11,000 seals on what is now a wildlife refuge.

Haast is the local centre for this remote country. State Highway 6 heads north along coastal plains through forests protected by the South West

◀ *LEFT: A lonely grave on the beach above Jackson Bay, the coastal road-end going south from Haast.*

◀ *OPPOSITE: The icy surface of the Fox Glacier challenges walking parties.*

◀ *PAGES 294–295: The Moeraki River runs from Lake Moeraki to the sea.*

New Zealand/Te Wahi Pounamu World Heritage Area (see page 271). These are the least damaged and most extensive lowland rainforests in New Zealand. Forests dominated by stands of kahikatea and rimu follow the rivers and shade the lower country. Kamahi clings to the hills with rata standing tall above the lower canopy. At colder elevations beech forests climb the alps.

At intervals along the highway short walks lead to viewpoints and interesting features of the forest. Knights Point carpark looks down on a seal colony. Lake Moeraki has track access to the coast where Fiordland crested penguins and yellow-eyed penguins share with other shorebirds and slumbering seals. Look also for the endangered southern crested grebe on the lakes left by glacial melting.

Lakes, notably Moeraki and Paringa, occupy valleys left by the ice-melt of vanished glaciers.

Occasionally, giant snow- and rain-fed rivers plunge down from the mountains. The lowland forests receive an annual rainfall of up to 5000 mm, but up in the alps the fall may be 14,000 mm. The steep, rock-strewn gorges and boulder riverbeds emphasise the wildness of this land; unstable, flash-flooding, slipping, and not to be trusted.

In places, behind the shingle shorelines, extensive lowland forest ridges run parallel to intervening wetlands. Until the end of the ice ages some of the glaciers reached out to this coast, and even now fall through dense forest down to 300 metres above sea level. The coastal sequence of parallel wetlands and forests has been built up by changing sea levels.

▲ TOP: Knights Point viewpoint, where the coastal road turns inland to Lake Moeraki. Seals settle on the beach below.

▲ ABOVE: A forest of rimu trees extends along the beach at Bruce Bay.

The glaciers that descend through the rainforest are the outstanding feature of the Westland/Tai Poutini National Park. The southernmost Fox Glacier falls from the back of Mt Tasman and other peaks of the Main Divide, in Aoraki/Mt Cook National Park. It descends through a narrowing valley for 13 kilometres to an altitude of around 300 metres above sea level. The Franz Josef Glacier, further north, falls 12 kilometres from an adjoining catchment.

Both glaciers fall steeply. In places the ice is 300 metres deep.

Heavy alpine storms bring snow, becoming ice to fuel the glacier. The glaciers then run in grinding streams taking around six years to descend to the rainforest.

Walking on a glacier reveals a mass of distorted and broken ice with crevasses and ridges along with the sound of

▲ TOP: *Kahikatea trees and flax grow in swamp forest by a coastal creek.*

▲ ABOVE: *On a pioneer farm, rata flowers in midsummer.*

subterranean water and occasional ice falls. The massive ice ridges up the glacier are created by variations in its rate of flow; the ice clinging to the valley sides is slowed by friction with the rock walls, but bellies forth in the centre where flow is relatively unimpeded. The tongue of the glacier is alive with falling blocks of ice collapsing, unpredictably, into the almost white-watered terminal lake. Small ice lumps float as 'icebergs', in time breaking up and bouncing downstream through the bush. Signs of glacial action in earlier times are carved into the walls of the vacated lower valleys, emphasising the erosive force of passing ice.

The death of an exploring ancestor is remembered in the Maori name of Fox Glacier, Te Moeka o Tuawe. Franz Josef is also known as Ka Roimata o Hine Hukatere, recalling the frozen tears of his lover. The occasionally steaming surface of the Waiho River, leaving Franz Josef Glacier, translates as 'smoking water'.

Further north, the Okarito Lagoon is a bird-rich estuary on the coast off SH6. Nearby Whataroa is the access point to visit the white heron/kotuku colony during the breeding season. From late October to the end of February guided tours depart for the Waitangiroto Scenic Reserve where white heron nest in the crowns of tree ferns or smaller trees overhanging the water. This is part of a kahikatea swamp and the only breeding site in New Zealand for this 'bird of a single flight'. The herons disperse throughout New Zealand after breeding but are most often seen along the south Westland coast.

Royal spoonbill make their home in the kahikatea trees in the Waitangiroto reserve too, but also breed elsewhere in

New Zealand. Cattle egrets migrate from Australia to the wetland waterways along the coast during autumn but only a few immatures spend the winter here.

The journey north continues to display the sequence of kahikatea swamps and rainforest but farming gradually takes over the flats. Much of this land was formerly forest, all of which is now protected.

Goldmining ghosts abound: some tent towns with populations of more than 2000 vanished overnight as news of a new find precipitated another goldrush. Other centres such as Ross and Hokitika survive, often with nineteenth-century buildings reflecting their origins and prosperity. In the late twentieth century several goldfields were reopened using modern equipment to reach alluvial gold.

While the road now follows the coastline and farms, the Southern Alps remain on the inland horizon. There are still the

DIFFERENT KIWI

Modern science using DNA tests has determined that the brown kiwi is arguably divisible into four species and possible subspecies.

The Okarito brown kiwi or kowi has a tiny population of around 120 compared with its North Island cousin.

The Haast brown kiwi or tokoeka also has a small population around 200–300.

The Stewart Island brown kiwi is most closely related to the brown kiwi of Fiordland just across Foveaux Strait.

The North Island brown kiwi in turn has several varieties.

▲ TOP: *The Arawhata River, one of the great west coast rivers which drain the Southern Alps.*

▲ ABOVE: *Kahikatea swamp forest reflected in a small lake.*

◀ OPPOSITE, TOP: *Franz Josef Glacier.*

◀ OPPOSITE, BOTTOM: *Fox Glacier.*

GREENSTONE/POUNAMU

Maori called the South Island Te Wai Pounamu, the waters of greenstone. This highly valued hard stone was used for weapons, tools and decoration.

Greenstone (poutini) was known as the fish of Ngahue, who took it south pursued by the goddess of grinding rocks who could cut through it. Other stories tell of Tama pursuing his wives, who were drowned or turned to stone in greenstone localities including the headwaters of Lake Wakatipu, Milford Sound, Jackson Bay and the Arahura/Taramakau rivers.

Geologically, greenstone is born from huge subterranean pressures forced by the rising of the Southern Alps. Lenses of this nephrite material have been excavated by the rivers and broken up. It can be hard to find as the outer layer often oxidises into a rough, whitish boulder with the greenstone hidden inside.

The stone comes in several forms, with colouring varying from practically opaque light green to shades of near black. Each type has its own name reflecting the colour and quality, among them: inanga (whitebait, a pale fish), kawakawa (after a dark-leaved sacred plant), and kahurangi (which is a cloudy stone).

The dark stone bowenite, found at Anita Bay and Poison Bay in Fiordland, is not strictly greenstone but its value was as high. It is known as tangiwai after the streaked tears that can be seen within if the stone is held to the light.

Pebbles of greenstone can still be found on West Coast beaches but all greenstone is legally the property of the Maori tribe, Ngai Tahu.

▲ *ABOVE: A vine form of rata which clambers over tree trunks or branches in rainforests. Various species flower in different hues at different seasons.*

rocky beds of snow-fed rivers to cross.

Some are sources of greenstone, a jade valued by Maori for the making of weapons, tools and personal adornment. This they traded across the alpine passes, to Canterbury and on to the North Island.

A major source was the Arahura River between Hokitika and Greymouth though nearby rivers also produce boulders.

The 'capital' of Westland is Greymouth, standing at the mouth of the Grey River. At the back of the town, the Grey flows through a narrow gorge cut between two ranges of hills. Travellers from here have a choice of journeys.

▲ *ABOVE AND LEFT:* *The popular view of the Southern Alps, reflected in still waters, is from Lake Matheson near the Fox Glacier settlement. On clear days New Zealand's two highest mountains can be seen reflected in the lake, with Tasman to the left and Aoraki/Mt Cook beyond, peeping over the Main Divide, at right. A walkway round the lake reveals the view and brings visitors close up to the birdlife of this sheltered water. Surrounding forests are dominated by tall kahikatea and rimu.*

KUMARA TO ARTHUR'S PASS

At Kumara Junction, the West Coast is linked to Canterbury by way of Arthur's Pass (SH73) and the Craigieburn high country (page 218–225). The features of Westland rainforest persist to the top of the pass with the summer spectacle of red-flowering rata in the darkness of the forest.

NORTH WESTLAND

The Paparoa Range runs for 47 kilometres, from Greymouth north along the coast, enclosing the Paparoa National Park.

This western coast is known for its giant surfs, biscuit-tin sunsets, and holiday hamlets. At first there are coal-mining townships, producing the bulk of New Zealand's bituminous coal. The ranges then rise sheer, up to 1200–1500 metres in places.

In the forested hills just south of Punakaiki, colonies of Westland black petrel are particularly active during winter. A population estimated at 2000–5000 nesting pairs feeds in the Tasman Sea, and off Cook Strait and the east coast. A threatened species, black petrel numbers grew with the hoki fishery offshore where they feed on scraps. In the evening birds can be seen flying in from sea.

Non-breeding birds make up the majority of the population which is estimated to be up to 9000 birds. Migratory, they visit Australian and Chathams waters, with reports from as far as South America. The birds return in later years to nest at age 12 at this one site.

Forests everywhere are a rich mixture of podocarps such as rimu and hardwoods. Higher on the ridges, above the river and on the slopes of the mountains, northern rata rises above the forest canopy, flowering a deep red in midsummer.

PANCAKE ROCKS

The Pancake Rocks are a landmark of the Paparoa National Park. Just off the road at Punakaiki, they stand up to 50 metres above boiling surf. Their appearance is sculpted by the wild waters of Dolomite Point, which have washed out alternating strata of mudstone and limestone, so what is left resembles stacks of pancakes. In rising seas the waters shoot up through blowholes and the air is thick with spume.

The surrounding landscape seems subtropical with groves of nikau palm growing near their southernmost limit, and coastal plants of warmer districts including kawakawa (northern pepper plant), and mamaku, the giant black tree fern. Streams run in deep valleys beneath limestone bluffs with frequent signs of cave systems below, including vanishing water and emerging pools. When it rains heavily in the Paparoa Ranges, rivers can rise swiftly and trap unprepared cavers in the underground galleries.

◀ *OPPOSITE: Heavy seas off the Tasman batter the limestone cliffs of Paparoa National Park. At Dolomite Point, Punakaiki, seas have collapsed a cavern and also feed blow holes.*

Walking is relatively easy in the low country, though the inland slopes of the Paparoa Range are for the experienced and well-prepared only.

The Paparoa coast is generally forested and there are a number of walks beneath overhanging cliffs and along reefs. The giant Miko Cliff, written of by early European explorers, was once on the main path along the coast and involved a vertiginous climb, by a rotting rope ladder made by Maori from rata vine with flax ties.

Flats north of Charleston were the sites for many goldrush claims in the 1860s. The land, known as pakihi, consists of low scrub and fern, and is often unfarmed. The problem is that the land sits on a pan of hard iron clay impervious to water. It is difficult to manage, or to find an economic way of carving through this barrier to create farmland.

A side road off SH6, south of Westport, diverts to the Tasman coast, giving alternative access to the large seal colony at Cape Foulwind then Carters Beach, continuing on to Westport on the Buller River (page 182).

North of Westport, SH67 follows a narrowing coastal plain beside the mountains. On the heights, huge coal measures form an undulating plateau in the clouds. Most of the mining settlements on the tops are ghost towns

▼ BELOW: *Erosion from the sea has carved the Pancake Rocks at Punakaiki into pillars of layered limestone. Blow holes play when the tide gets high and rough.*

now. A few steep and winding roads still run up the hills but the sheer gravity-powered railway to Denniston remains only an historic ruin. Mining continues on an industrial scale atop the subalpine Stockton Plateau, however.

After turning inland to round the high bluffs of the Radiant Range, the road to Karamea is narrow. Arms of Kahurangi National Park stretch down from the heights of the mountains of northwest Nelson and human settlement is restricted to the coastal plains and valleys about Karamea.

People who cross Kahurangi National Park by way of the Heaphy Track emerge 15 kilometres north of Karamea in a land of warm, wet forests where nikau palms flourish. (The time taken to walk from

▷ TOP RIGHT: *The limestone bluffs of the Paparoa National Park are worn by water. Cave systems riddle the eroded gorges.*

▷ ABOVE RIGHT: *Coal deposits are extensive along the ranges overlooking the sea north of Westport. While some famous fields are now abandoned, coal mining remains an important industry, with extensive opencast mining on the Stockton Plateau.*

▷ RIGHT: *Caving opportunities in the limestone country are many and varied, including beginners' caves in Paparoa National Park.*

Aorere in Golden Bay to the track end on the beach north of Karamea is four to five days over a distance of 85 kilometres.) There are short, local walks into the nikau groves at the exit from the track.

The major wilderness feature is closer to Karamea, however; a complex of limestone caves and underground streams at Oparara. Again accessed by rough gravel road, the Oparara basin contains caves and remnant limestone arches surrounded by mature forests of rimu and kahikatea.

The Honeycomb Hill caves contain the remains of vanished birds such as the extinct moa. Entry is by guided tour only.

◀ TOP LEFT: *Waters in the Oparara system run through limestone caves and sinkholes.*

◀ BOTTOM LEFT: *Weka or woodhen are common along the northern West Coast. They come close to people in some stopping places and are adept at stealing bright trifles from the picnic rug. Feeding mainly on vegetable matter, they also take insects and small creatures such as worms and spiders; they even rob the nests of other ground-nesting birds.*

▶ OPPOSITE: *The warm microclimates of the West Coast allow for the southernmost occurences of a few subtropical plants. Nikau, the southern palm, is a feature of the coastal Paparoa National Park.*

ON THE ROAD
IN NEW ZEALAND

Motoring in back-country New Zealand can be demanding for anyone used to sealed highways. Even main roads can be rough in places with unexpected potholes and damage from roadworks. Road edges are often soft-shouldered and care should be taken when pulling off the seal to take pictures etc.

Heavy rain and local flooding can cause

▲ TOP AND ABOVE: *New Zealand road signs follow the international system of warnings and directions. There are a few special extras such as those for stock movements and warnings to look out for kiwi on the road at night.*

slips and washouts in any season. Even major state highways may be closed occasionally by snow or floods — in key places conspicuous signboards usually advise on the condition of main routes between regions so alternatives may be followed.

Roads in more remote places may still have a shingle surface, with loose gravel, unexpected potholes and corrugations in places. The major problem is the loose surface where shingle builds up on a narrow road between clear road surfaces. The centre strip is then shared by vehicles going in both directions. When pulling left to pass opposing traffic a vehicle may skid on the shingle strips. Having the vehicle's speed under control, with a margin for a quick stop, is vital in these conditions. Speeds should be continually adjusted to the road conditions.

Occasionally roads may be blocked by herds of cattle or sheep. There is a golden rule here: stop. Don't toot. Put the vehicle in first gear and allow it to make its own way through the mob at the slowest speed possible. Usually farmers and their dogs won't help you. Frightening as it may feel at first, a placid flock of beasts will slowly move aside around your vehicle, allowing you to proceed through.

Allow additional time for country journeys — it is impossible and undesirable to make the speed limit a target speed, as the regular warning signs about safe-cornering speeds indicate. Rest briefly every hour: it's hard work handling some roads, and on others it is a challenge to stay awake. A cup of coffee and a few stretches can help.

Another worthwhile precaution in the countryside is keeping the fuel tank topped up. It can sometimes be a long way between petrol and diesel pumps, and in country districts selling fuel is not a round-the-clock business.

Carry a cellphone for emergencies, with a hands-free kit if you want to call from the car. Using a cellphone while driving is illegal. In some areas 555 reaches traffic patrols, and 111 is the national emergency number for all police, fire and ambulance. It is a serious offence to leave the scene of, or fail to report involvement in, an injury accident. Cellphone coverage is widespread in New Zealand though there are many shadow areas and it may be easiest to call from an elevated position. Leave the phone on and it will transmit an audible signal when you re-enter an effective coverage area.

Not every parking place is safe. Notices at many tourist parking areas warn of local thieves. Park when possible alongside other vehicles or where there is frequently passing foot traffic or a local stall-keeper. Keep valuables out of sight; better still don't leave items like cameras, passports and jewellery in the vehicle.

When pulling off the road for the night, park with other vehicles, preferably in a proper camping ground or trailer park. Perhaps choose motels and hotels which provide secure parking, for convenience, or unload valuables overnight. New Zealand is generally a law-abiding country, but tourists are a tempting target, particularly in depressed rural areas.

Don't be put off though. People who are informed of the risks can generally minimise them by taking these precautions.

Joining the Automobile Association is a relatively inexpensive insurance, even for visitors. Besides the range of complimentary travel guides and maps there is also the wonderful 'rescue' service which can bring a roadside mechanic or rescue vehicle to your aid in an emergency.

WATCHING
NEW ZEALAND BIRDS

New Zealand is often referred to as the 'Land of Birds' but in fact not many more than 300 species have been recorded here. The title is deserved, however, because birds occupied the land without competition from mammals till Maori arrived 800–1000 years ago. Consequently birds occupied many of the niches occupied elsewhere by mammals. It was the nature of New Zealand's birds — many of which dwelt on the ground or were weak fliers — that excited the first birdwatchers.

Many birdwatchers from overseas come to see the rare and endangered species increasingly to be found in the open sanctuaries being developed on offshore islands. Others delight in the range of birds which may be seen in towns, gardens, parks and waterways, as well as the forests.

Birdwatching may begin at home with a bird feeding-table or bird bath adjacent to the house. A lot can be learned about bird behaviour round sources of food and water. Birds may also be observed en masse in breeding colonies (gannets, gulls, terns, shags or cormorants) or at migration sites (seashore birds from the northern hemisphere, etc.).

Getting close to birds involves the ability to sit still and let the birds come to you. Most bird photographs are taken from portable hides. A motor car can be a good 'hide', parked by a lakeside or at the edge of the bush. The late naturalist and photographer Geoff Moon has suggested you'll see more forest birds by sitting quietly in the bush for an hour than if you go actively hunting them.

Smaller forest birds, such as robins and fantails, can be attracted closer by the use of a 'squeak bottle'. Rub a little piece of polystyrene on the glass and inquisitive birds will come closer. Use of squeak bottles and other bird lures is discouraged in many places, however, as it may disturb territorial birds, particularly in the nesting season. For similar reasons, the use of tape recordings should be limited to attempts to capture birds for translocations and breeding purposes, under scientific direction.

NATIVE & INTRODUCED BIRDS

Introductions, natural and deliberate, have helped shape the present nature of New Zealand's birdlife.

ENDEMIC BIRDS are peculiar to New Zealand, or parts of it, and are believed to have evolved here.

NATIVE BIRDS are the result of self-introductions to New Zealand over the millennia, but they also exist in other countries, as species or subspecies.

INTRODUCED BIRDS, an additional one-fifth of New Zealand's bird species, have been deliberately introduced by European settlers.

ENDEMIC BIRDS particularly interest visiting birdwatchers. Most 'endemics' are primitive forms, often flightless or weak fliers. They occur in most bird classifications though some, like the extinct moa, are unique. Endemics include a number of forest birds, along with the wrybill plover with its beak twisting to the right, various Chatham Island species and subspecies, and our native parrots.

NATIVE BIRDS are also found in other countries in a closely related form and include the white heron, cattle egret, kingfisher, various gulls and terns, the harrier, fantail, silvereye, and several duck species. Several common species of birds found their own way here during the twentieth century, including white-faced heron, welcome swallow and spur-winged plover. Self-introduced birds are immediately protected with the status of native birds.

The native pukeko is believed to be a self-introduced species. Known elsewhere as the purple gallinule, this cosmopolitan species probably represents a later evolution from an ancestral species — one which evolved here separately into the notornis or takahe.

The **INTRODUCED BIRDS** of New Zealand come largely from Europe, brought in for sentimental or sporting reasons, or to control insect pests. They include the common house sparrow, the European song thrush, the blackbird, starling and a range of finches, along with the traditional field game birds. A few escaped cage birds have also established in the wild.

WHERE BIRDS LIVE

FAMILIAR BIRDS OF GARDENS AND PARKS. Mature suburbs and town parks often replicate the richest of bird habitats — the forest edge. Here may be found the common bush birds and most of the introduced species. Encourage them by providing their essential needs: food, water and shelter. A bird bath or a bird feeder close to the house is a great place to observe bird behaviour. Sheltering shrubs and hedges may encourage insect-eating birds, and provide some with places to nest. (Cats must be discouraged.) Resident birds often include the introduced house sparrow, thrush, blackbird, and various finches, along with native birds such as the silvereye, grey warbler, fantail, tui and bellbird. Where there is water — a stream, a pond, a marshy area — birds from those environments may also occur. Town lakes can attract a broad range of ducks, dabchick, pukeko, shags and gulls. Generally, these birds are more used to people and can be more closely observed.

LOCAL PECULIARITIES. Escaped cage birds have established local populations, particularly in northern New Zealand. The Australian eastern rosella is widespread in forest and towns from the Bay of Plenty northward. In the Auckland region, both Indian spotted doves and ring-neck doves frequent gardens and parks. The Indian mynah has spread through most North Island districts. Bellbirds, common in some districts, vanished from the Auckland region and northward in the nineteenth century while persisting on offshore islands. The introduced little owl frequents the drier eastern South Island and in places has largely replaced the native morepork owl.

NORTHERN & SOUTHERN SPECIES. The end of the last ice age separated the North and South Island bird populations. Regional subspecies developed, notably of kaka and kokako, but also the extinct native thrush, bush robin and pied tit. A black phase of the pied fantail is found only in the South Island; the whitehead occurs only in the North. The South Island also has species not found elsewhere: the mountain parrot kea, the black-fronted tern, yellowhead and brown creeper. Cook Strait also marks the northern limit of some penguins.

FOREST BIRDS. Native forest is the home of many species which have developed a dependency on it. Introduced pests, such as possums and stoats, have devastated many of these populations, bringing a number of birds close to extinction. Birds often live at different levels in the forest. At and near ground level, fantail, bush robin and tit are easily observable. Whitehead and rifleman may feed on lower tree trunks. Parrots and parakeets live in the tree tops but may descend into the fabric of the forest to feed. Yellowhead/mohua and brown creeper tend to live in the forest canopy. Treetop birds are hardest to locate. (It's a good idea to learn the

calls from a commercial recording and listen for them.)

OVERSEAS (FOREST) MIGRANTS. The shining cuckoo and the long-tailed cuckoo arrive from the tropical Pacific in spring and breed in the nests of others over summer. Shining cuckoo lay in the nests of grey warbler which occur widely, while long-tailed cuckoo tend to favour deeper forest because their hosts are whitehead in the North Island and yellowhead and brown creeper in the South Island. Both cuckoos are hard to observe as they throw their voices like a ventriloquist.

ALPINE BIRDS. Kea, the mountain parrot of the South Island high country, may be encountered looking for scraps at roadside rest spots as well as screeching in flight high overhead. The native falcon usually lives among the crags and hunts the forest tops for small birds. The diminutive rock wren is present only in remnant populations gravely diminished by carnivorous pests.

WETLAND BIRDS. These are easiest observed on lakeshores and the margins of swamps. In spring watch for breeding behaviour and the feeding of young by birds which variously dive or dabble for their food. Most ducks, herons and swans are easy to approach but there is a range of more secretive species which tend to hide in reed beds and are more often heard than seen. These include the bittern (which communicates with a low booming sound), fernbird and the crakes.

COASTAL BIRDS. Variable oyster-catchers, and New Zealand dotterel (in the north) breed in summer on open beaches just above the high-tide mark. Colonies of the various terns and gulls may also establish on sandspits. (They also use the broad shingle riverbeds of the eastern South Island.) Clifftops and coastal trees may be home to colonies of the various shag (cormorant) species.

SEASHORE BIRDS. From spring to autumn, in particular, New Zealand's shallow harbours and estuaries are home to thousands of wading birds, many of them seasonal migrants from the Asian and North American tundras (36 recorded species). They come to New Zealand in the summer to fatten up for their breeding cycle in subarctic conditions. Godwit and knot form spectacular flocks; along with them are local species, the pied oystercatcher, pied stilt and wrybill plover in season. Watch for them at roosting places when the birds are driven off the mudflats by the rising tide.

INTERNAL MIGRANTS. Some seashore birds migrate between the North and South Islands to breed. Both the wrybill and the South Island pied oystercatcher breed inland about the South Island shingle riverbeds in late winter, then migrate largely to the great northern harbours in summer. Other birds such as pied stilt (in summer) and kingfisher (in winter) may move more locally from inland districts to be near the seacoast. Gannets and white-fronted terns are species which spend some of their youth on Australian shores but return to New Zealand to breed.

OCEAN BIRDS. New Zealand's position in the Roaring Forties makes it a great place to observe pelagic birds, including migratory shearwaters and petrels, skuas and albatrosses. More than 30 different species of petrels and shearwaters breed on our offshore islands. Pelagic birds feed with the whales off Kaikoura. Specialist boat operators offer ocean bird tours.

RARE & ENDANGERED BIRDS. Wild populations of some birds, such as kakapo and takahe, are restricted to 'no go' management areas. A number of notable species, including takahe, saddleback, stitchbird, kiwi and parakeet may be observed in captivity, usually as an adjunct of 'captive-breeding' programmes. They are better observed, however, in open sanctuaries such as Tiritiri Matangi Island off Auckland, and Kapiti Island off the Wellington west coast, where pest-free reserves have encouraged the re-release of endangered birds into more natural conditions.

OCEAN ISLAND GROUPS. Millions of seabirds breed about the Subantarctic World Heritage Area, the island groups to the south of New Zealand. Brief landings can be made by ocean tour parties at a few of them. The more accessible Chatham Islands group has several species and subspecies found nowhere else.

PLACES TO GO

- Birdwatchers could begin at home, or choose the habitat they're most interested in to find particular birds. As some birds move with the seasons, check that the time (or the tide) is appropriate first.

- The best places to watch birds are generally in the wild; in areas of the national and conservation parks which cover more than a third of New Zealand.

- 'Mainland islands' comprise discrete areas where intensive pest control allows the survival of sensitive and vulnerable bird species on the mainland. The more accessible public places include Trounson Kauri Park (Northland), Boundary Stream (inland Hawke's Bay), and St Arnaud (Nelson Lakes National Park). Private and trust initiatives include: Karori Wildlife Sanctuary, Zealandia, 250 hectares fenced off against pests and only 10 minutes from Parliament Buildings in Wellington; Forest and Bird's Bushy Park near Kai Iwi out of Whanganui; and Maungatautari mountain in South Waikato, where the local community has ring-fenced 3400 hectares around the forested summit.

OTHER AREAS INCLUDE:

- Offshore islands where pest control is recreating original conditions. The open sanctuary of Tiritiri Matangi Island near Auckland is the showplace with saddleback, stitchbird, kiwi, notornis/takahe, parakeets and other native forest birds. Kapiti near Wellington is another accessible island sanctuary with similar birds plus kaka. A range of other islands under restoration may be accessible from time to time: check with the Department of Conservation.

- Northern harbours for shorebirds and migrant waders, particularly the Miranda Shorebird Centre which has hides and accommodation on the Firth of Thames in the Auckland region, and the Manukau Harbour coastal walkways, Auckland.

- The Hauraki Gulf or Bay of Plenty by special tourist boats for pelagic birds.

- The lower Waikato lakes for wetland birds, but access to the shores is limited.

- The Rotorua Lakes for wetland birds, particularly the wildlife sanctuary in Sulphur Bay and the shores of Lake Okareka; Mokoia Island has saddleback and weka.

- Gannet colonies at Muriwai Regional Park, Auckland, and Cape Kidnappers near Napier.

- Pukaha/Mount Bruce National Wildlife Centre, a Department of Conservation breeding centre in the Wairarapa, with kiwi, kokako, stitchbird, takahe, kaka, kakariki and black teal.

- Mouth of the Manawatu River near Foxton, for shorebirds.

- Farewell Spit, a conducted tourist trip past tidal flats and ground-nesting gannets.

- Motuara Island, by boat from Picton; forest birds including saddleback, and an endemic king shag colony.

- Kaikoura coast: albatrosses, petrels and shearwaters on a guided boat tour.

- Avon–Heathcote Estuary, and oxidation ponds, Christchurch.

- Otago Peninsula: royal albatross colony, yellow-eyed penguin.

- The Catlins district of Southland: forest birds and penguins.

- Stewart Island: night walks for kiwi; Ulva Island forest bird sanctuary.

- Many zoos and private bird parks have permits to keep native birds in captivity, and are variously involved in endangered bird breeding programmes. While these programmes are not usually on display, these parks may be of interest to travelling birdwatchers seeking up-to-date information on species.

- Watch also for local initiatives, such as the blue penguin walk in Oamaru, and local Forest and Bird reserves. Visitor Information Centres usually carry brochures for community and privately owned reserves open to the public.

TECHNIQUES

Binoculars are an essential tool for the birdwatcher. The ideal format is 8x30, giving eight times magnification and a good wide field of vision. Higher magnifications are physically larger and harder to hold steady. (The 7x50 binoculars are heavier and of lower magnification but may be easier for watching birds from an unsteady boat.) Glasses should function well in low light, with a minimum of colour distortion, and be capable of focusing on birds which are close to you. Watching shorebirds out over the tidal flats may require a telescope but the birds will come to you at high-tide roosts.

For close-up observation, hides can be useful. A small tent-like structure (which does not flap in the wind) is set up in an area frequented by birds. Most birds can't count so, provided an assistant accompanies the observer out to the hide and returns once the observer is in place, birds generally assume the hide to be empty. Of course the pretence must be maintained; the assistant must return to collect the observer from the hide.

A motor vehicle can serve as a good hide if parking near the birds won't disturb them or damage the environment. Keep movement inside to a minimum and birds often approach quite close.

Cameras suitable for bird photography need to be capable of taking shots at high shutter speeds to freeze movement, with interchangeable lenses for close and distant work. There are no laws in New Zealand directly prohibiting the photography of rare species but disturbance of all native species is prohibited and there is a large ethical concern to avoid disturbing them. Nest photography can easily alarm birds and cause them to abandon the nest. Expert bird photographers may advance a hide towards a nest over several days, depending on their knowledge of species. If you must do this, read widely and ask experts, then practise on common introduced garden birds.

AGENCIES & ENTHUSIASTS GROUPS

Ornithological Society of New Zealand, PO Box 12-397, Wellington. Learned society with many lay members; regional groups hold lectures and conduct surveys of birds. Publishes the journal *Notornis*, quarterly *Southern Birds* and popular newsletters. Website: www. osnz.org.nz

Forest and Bird (Royal Forest and Bird Protection Society of New Zealand Inc,) PO Box 631, Wellington. Conservation society with more than 40 branches nationwide; organises trips and talks, quarterly colour magazine *Forest & Bird*, adult and junior groups, local conservation and restoration. Website: www.forestandbird.org.nz

Miranda Naturalists' Trust, RD3, Pokeno, South Auckland. Membership organisation operating the Miranda Shorebird Centre on the Firth of Thames. The centre of migratory and shorebird studies, with public hides, volunteer guides, occasional residential courses, visitor accommodation. Email: shorebird@xtra.co.nz

Ducks Unlimited New Zealand Inc, PO Box 9795, Newmarket, Auckland. Membership organisation focusing on wetland restoration and breeding wetland birds. Quarterly magazine *Flight*, local projects, occasional field trips and social occasions.

Department of Conservation, PO Box 10–420, Wellington, with regional management offices and a network of local field centres. Government department responsible for protecting wildlife, managing national parks and reserves, does scientific research into birdlife, breeding, management etc. Website: www.doc.govt.nz

Universities and larger museums employ bird scientists and conduct research.

Commercial tours and guides list at www. birdingnz.co.nz

Most localities maintain a website.

FURTHER READING

New Zealand has an extensive literature relating to its environment and nature. Some of the most authoritative volumes are listed here but there are many more which deal with single subjects, some as specialised as insect-eating plants, orchids or fungi. There are also regional titles which study a locality in detail.

Many guidebooks to species are available in popular form from general publishers such as Reed, Penguin, Bateman and New Holland, and from specialists such as Godwit and The Bush Press.

BIRDS

Reader's Digest Complete Book of New Zealand Birds, C.J.R. Robertson, consultant editor (Reader's Digest, Sydney, 1985). Sometimes dated text but good field pictures and general notes.

New Zealand Birds: A Locality Guide, Stuart Chambers (Arun Books). A detailed guide to birding sites throughout New Zealand, with an illustrated species guide.

The Field Guide to the Birds of New Zealand, Barrie D. Heather & Hugh A. Robertson (Viking, Auckland). The official guide produced for the Ornithological Society of New Zealand and frequently revised.

Bird books by the naturalist and photographer Geoff Moon generally feature fine behavioural photography along with his valued field notes on many species.

PLANTS

The Native Trees of New Zealand, J.T. Salmon (Reed, Auckland, 1980). A big and copiously illustrated guide to New Zealand trees showing young and mature specimens, flowers, fruit and diagnostic detail, in layperson's terms.

GEOLOGY AND LANDFORMS

Landforms: The Shaping of New Zealand, Les Molloy & Roger Smith (Craig Potton Publishing, Nelson, 2002). Map-makers' images of New Zealand from the air, digitally enhanced to emphasise landforms, with straightforward notes about the underlying geology and processes which have shaped the landscape.

*The Reed Field Guide to New Zealand Geology: An Introduction to Rocks, Minerals and Fossil*s, Jocelyn Thornton (Reed, Auckland, 2002). Place-based description of New Zealand's geological features.

Trilobites, Dinosaurs and Moa Bones: The Story of New Zealand Fossils, Bruce Hayward (Bush Press, Auckland, 1985). Straightforward account of New Zealand's geology, as recorded in its fossils, with a guide to finding them.

Delving Deeper: Half a Century of Cave Discovery in New Zealand, Moira Lipyeat & Les Wright (Hazard Press, Christchurch, 2003). Recounts the exploration of New Zealand's cave systems.

Geological Society *Guidebooks*; the Geological Society of New Zealand publishes several field guides to interesting localities and suggests tours. Current coverage is listed on its website www.gsnz.org.nz and books are available by mail order. See, in particular, *Geyserland* (Rotorua district) and *Central Rocks* (inland Otago) which are generally available in those regions too.

NATURAL HISTORY

Ghosts of Gondwana: The History of Life in New Zealand, George Gibbs (Craig Potton, Nelson, 2006). An accessible account of the formation of the New Zealand archipelago, describing the evolution of its plants and animals, over the 80 million years since this land drifted away from the ancestral continent of Gondwana.

Craig Potton has written, photographed and published a number of stunning pictorial albums with explanatory text focusing on natural regions (*Yesterday's New Earth*), Tongariro, Paparoa (*Images from a Limestone Landscape*, with Andy Dennis) and Aoraki/Mt Cook.

Forests, Fiords and Glaciers: New Zealand's World Heritage was published by the Royal Forest and Bird Protection Society in 1987 to make the case for a World Heritage Area over the southernmost national parks.

Wetlands of New Zealand: A Bitter-Sweet Story, Janet Hunt (Random House, Auckland, 2007). Wetlands, including waterways, once covered an estimated 20 percent of New Zealand's land area; now that figure is less than 2 percent, as noted in this well-illustrated book.

For handbooks and charts, look for anything by Andrew Crowe, including colour guides to spiders, insects, plants and shells, some in life-size versions for use in the field. (Penguin, Auckland.)

NATIONAL PARKS

National Parks and Other Wild Places of New Zealand, Kathy Ombler (New Holland, Auckland, 2001). A well-illustrated, popular account of the national parks, plus some of New Zealand's larger conservation parks.

PESTS AND WEEDS

Pests and Weeds: A Blueprint for Action, Kevin Hackwell & Geoff Bertram (New Zealand Conservation Authority, Wellington, 1999). Summarises the impact of introduced animals and weeds on New Zealand and estimates the economic costs.

LOCAL GUIDES

There are many excellent books, usually only available locally. Some favourites:

AUCKLAND

A Field Guide to Auckland: Exploring the Region's Natural and Historic Heritage, Ewen Cameron, Bruce Hayward & Graeme Murdoch (Godwit, Auckland, 1997). Broad-ranging trip guide to 140 places around Auckland and the Hauraki Gulf, including the rocks and landforms, plants and animals, plus local and Maori history. Excellent, all round.

A Natural History of Auckland, edited by John Morton (David Bateman & the Auckland Regional Council, 1993). Experts describe the region in popular terms, from its geology to its modern ecology, including its plants and birds, the seashores and islands.

Tiritiri Matangi, Anne Rimmer (Tandem, Auckland 2004). The story of the 'open sanctuary' island in the Hauraki Gulf where visitors can see such rarities as takahe in the wild.

Waitakere Ranges, Ranges of Inspiration: Nature, History, Culture, edited by Bruce & Trixie Harvey (Waitakere Ranges Protection Society Inc., 2006). A celebratory volume; huge, highly detailed, and exhaustive.

TARANAKI

The Story of Egmont National Park (Department of Conservation, c.1987). Revised reprint of a former national park guide.

WELLINGTON

Kapiti, Chris Maclean (The Whitcombe Press, 1999). A highly detailed examination in text and pictures of the famous bird sanctuary.

CANTERBURY

From Tussocks to Tourists: The Story of the Central Canterbury High Country, David Relph (Canterbury University Press, Christchurch 2007). A well-illustrated record of nature and the effects of settlement on the wild tussocklands.

Wild Rivers: Discovering the Natural History of the Central South Island, Neville Peat & Brian Patrick (Otago University Press, Dunedin, 2001). Explores the nature of inland South Canterbury, notably the Mackenzie country, the mountains and the braided rivers down to the coast, from the Rangitata mouth to coastal North Otago.

OTAGO AND SOUTHLAND

The Natural History of Southern New Zealand, edited by John Darby, R. Ewan Fordyce, Alan Mark, Keith Probert & Colin Townsend (Otago University Press, Dunedin, 2003). A comprehensive and well-illustrated account by numerous experts of the nature and habitats of New Zealand, south of the Waitaki River (and Jackson Bay in Westland).

Wild Dunedin and *Wild Central* (Otago University Press, Dunedin). Two of a series by Neville Peat and Brian Patrick 'discovering the natural history' of the wider Dunedin area and central Otago. Another volume, *Wild Fiordland*, examines the nature of Fiordland. Neville Peat has also written a similar introduction to Stewart Island/ Rakiura National Park.

INDEX

Page numbers in **bold** refer to illustrations

The author thanks the Department of Conservation for the use of the following photographs: bottlenose dolphin (SKF Ericson, 1994), page 67; South Island saddleback (Dick Veitch, 1979), page 171; Hector's dolphin (Erin Green, 2004), page 209; kaki/black stilt (Dick Veitch), page 229; little blue penguin (Rosalind Cole, 2000), page 244; northern royal albatross (AE Wright, 1969), page 263; all Crown Copyright, Department of Conservation. Thanks also to Tony and Jenny Enderby for the photograph of Goat Island, page 44.

A RANDOM HOUSE BOOK published by Random House New Zealand
18 Poland Road, Glenfield, Auckland, New Zealand

For more information about our titles go to www.randomhouse.co.nz

A catalogue record for this book is available from the National Library of New Zealand

Random House New Zealand is part of the Random House Group
New York   London   Sydney   Auckland   Delhi   Johannesburg

First published 2010

Design: Sarah Elworthy
Printed in China through Bookbuilders